Agendashift:

Outcome-oriented change and continuous transformation

Mike Burrows

Foreword by Daniel Mezick

Published by New Generation Publishing in 2018

Copyright © Mike Burrows 2018

First Edition

ISBN: 1-78719-726-8

ISBN-13: 978-1-78719-726-8

www.newgeneration-publishing.com

 New Generation Publishing

To Sharon

Contents

Foreword iii

Introduction 1

Background and audience 3

Improvement, change, and continuous transformation 5

Navigating Agendashift 6

Chapter 1. Discovery 11

The Celebration (5W) 11

The True North exercise: Everyone able to work consistently at their best 13

15-minute FOTO 15

Review, revise, and organise 21

Behind the scenes 23

Key points – 1. Discovery... 29

Chapter 2. Exploration 31

The Agendashift delivery assessment, mini edition...................... 32

Debriefing a survey 35

Agreement on action areas 42

Organise your outcomes with the Four Points exercise............. 45

Agreement on scope 56

Behind the scenes 57

Key points – 2. Exploration.. 63

Chapter 3. Mapping 67

The spine of our plan: A transformation journey...................... 68

Visualising your transformation map..................................... 76

Review and reconcile... 78

Choose what's next 79

Behind the scenes 81

Key points – 3. Mapping 87

Chapter 4. Elaboration 89

Options thinking...90

Hypothesis-driven change 93

Alternative approaches...103

Allow your thinking to be tested 104

Behind the scenes 105

Key points – 4. Elaboration 109

Chapter 5. Operation 111

Five principles of 21st century change leadership.........................112

A change of focus...115

Managing your experiments 120

Towards continuous transformation (prompts 13-18).................128

Where to start? 135

Behind the scenes 141

Key points – 5. Operation...147

Epilogue: The Full Circle exercise 149

Resources 151

Resources mentioned in this book 151

The Agendashift partner programme 151

Other resources 152

Acknowledgements 153

About the author 155

Index 157

Foreword

It's a good thing Agendashift is now here. The pace of change, driven by software technology, is transforming the world of work in a rather abrupt way. Businesses that cannot adapt quickly find themselves under pressure from those who actually can. Progressive business leaders now need innovative new tools: methods for navigating and coping with continuous change.

Agendashift is such a tool. A deep integration of many useful elements in a clear, 5-step process, Agendashift is an impressive piece of culture technology. "Culture tech" includes designed meeting formats, designed workflow frameworks, and designed interaction protocols. These elements facilitate clear thinking and communication while encouraging real agreement at scale across the whole enterprise. Tools like these help teams, divisions and entire enterprises to thrive, by increasing the quality of interactions, in service to great outcomes. Agendashift is an excellent example of one of these tools.

One striking aspect of Agendashift is the inherently engaging nature of the process. Employee engagement is absolutely essential for rapid and lasting change. This is so important that a new type of culture technology called Engagement Models is now emerging. Agendashift is kind of engagement model. It represents a way to naturally engage every employee, at every level, in the process of change. Part framework and part engagement model, Agendashift is a rich composition of culture technology tools, a composition that forms a complete system. A system that facilitates real improvement - not just quick fixes, but changes of a more challenging kind, brought to life by people engaged in the process and invested in outcomes that they helped to articulate.

If you are a business leader looking for tools that facilitate real change in real organizations, this is your book. As you read it, realize that Agendashift represents a new kind of tool for a new kind of executive leader. In the new world of work, executives create the conditions for employee engagement and innovation, in service to great business outcomes. To make this happen, pioneering leaders will use new tools. Culture technology tools.

Tools like Agendashift.

Daniel Mezick

www.DanielMezick.com
Author, The Culture Game
Co-Author, The OpenSpace Agility Handbook
Guilford, CT, USA
March 14, 2018

Introduction

If the line "a humane, *start with what you do now* approach to change" sounds familiar, chances are you've read my first book, *Kanban from the Inside*. In case you haven't read it (don't worry, it's not a prerequisite for this one), you should know that I devoted several chapters to techniques for understanding *what you do now* from a range of different perspectives. Clearly, I was very attached to the *start with what you do now* principle. I still am!

Contrast that with another well-known principle, habit #2 of Stephen Covey's 7 Habits: *Begin with the end in mind*. The funny thing? That's a great principle to hold too.

The apparent tension between *start with what you do now* and *begin with the end in mind* isn't hard to resolve: we just have to accept that the latter isn't about the design of solutions but is instead about the outcomes we want to achieve. This acceptance can be liberating:

- It's ok not to have all the answers right away

- It's ok to allow your solutions to evolve in response to or in anticipation of changing conditions and needs

- It's ok to be sceptical of people who – with no respect for your particular context – show little interest in understanding but are still quick with their prescriptions

- It's ok to end up with solutions that you wouldn't read in any textbook

With this kind of interpretation, the two principles complement each other well:

1. *Start with what you do now* is about the present – the realities staff and customers experience each working day, what makes

those experiences good, bad, or indifferent, and the extent to which people's needs are met

2. *Begin with the end in mind* is about the future – encouraging us to engage the imagination and find some clarity of purpose

This book is designed to help you help your organisation bring these two perspectives together in ways that help bring about lasting change. It describes a set of interconnected tools and a participatory process that invites people to dig deep together to discover shared ambitions, identify obstacles to those ambitions, find agreement on meaningful outcomes, and follow through systematically.

Over the course of its evolution we have variously described Agendashift as "values-based", "inclusive", "non-prescriptive", and "framework-agnostic". We have since found better ways to describe it, but to begin to understand what makes it different, here are a few things that it is not:

- It is not what I would call a 20th century change management approach, which is to say one that concerns itself with *overcoming resistance* to predetermined changes
- It is not tied to a single delivery framework (Agile or otherwise) , concerned with adherence to a prescribed set of practices
- It is not over-reliant on mechanistic, process-based views of how organisations work

Agendashift is indeed a change management approach, but instead of expecting and dealing with resistance, it helps practitioners and sponsors alike to proceed with genuine openness and to include people in a process of co-creation. Instead of prescription, Agendashift is *generative* in nature, stimulating people to generate a range of appropriate options in context, and then to collaborate on their implementation. And whilst we fully appreciate the importance of process, we're as likely to focus on the quality and timing of conversations and the values that drive decision making as we are on formal process design.

These are all good differentiators, but most important is *"outcome-oriented"*, outcomes and agreement on outcomes being absolutely central to Agendashift. I'm not referring to generalised claims about the benefits of using Agendashift. Rather, outcomes are Agendashift's main currency. Every exercise you will encounter in this book in some way elicits or works with outcomes of several kinds:

- Ambitions, aspirations, strategic goals
- Intermediate objectives – elements of strategy, milestones, and other signs of significant progress
- The impact (hoped-for or observed) of experiments and other forms of action
- The end result when needs are met

Outcomes such as these are everywhere of course, but it's very easy to lose sight of them. We fall in love not only with solutions, but their delivery vehicles! Our hope is that Agendashift's deliberate attention to outcomes will help organisations and practitioners achieve their goals more effectively.

Background and audience

Broadly, Agendashift should be seen as a product of the Lean-Agile community. Almost by definition, this is a community that likes to celebrate Lean and Agile both separately and together, recognising both the individual contributions and the mutual synergies of these two great movements. Respect for the principles and values that underpin both bodies of knowledge allows a diverse community rich in specific expertise to avoid descending into factionalism (well, most of the time, anyway).

Agendashift's conscious avoidance of prescription might resonate with many members of the Lean-Agile community, but the unfortunate truth is that too many Lean, Agile, and even Lean-Agile initiatives still demonstrate a decidedly 20th century approach to change. Sometimes we are left wondering what happened to Lean and Agile values, *"respect for people"* and *"People and interactions over processes and tools"* falling by the wayside in the blinkered pursuit of framework adoption, imposed top-down.

We are just as disheartened when transformation efforts are timid or directionless, lacking in meaningful engagement, over-relying on change happening bottom-up, more out of hope than realistic expectation or deliberate action. Whether it's too much of the wrong kind of ambition or too little, some of Agendashift's outcome-orientation is sorely needed.

Some might worry that our stance of non-prescription implies that we're against the use of frameworks. Let me put minds at rest: Frameworks – Scrum being the best-known example of an Agile process framework – are vital sources not just of tried-and-tested tools but of knowledge, experience, passion, and inspiration. If you are familiar with a framework and that framework offers a path beyond a current organisational obstacle, then of course you should take advantage. If Agendashift is what helps you seize that opportunity, then both are working precisely as they should. We hope also that you feel helped rather than threatened when Agendashift encourages people to step outside comfort zones and consider alternative or novel solutions.

Whatever your background, read this book if any of the following apply:

- You'd like to see a model for 21st century change leadership, and how that might inform your work as coach, consultant, or some other kind of change agent

- You've a more specific interest – whether as a practitioner or potential sponsor – in Lean-Agile change (perhaps under a banner of "Agile transformation", "Agile adoption", or similar)

- You'd love to see a model for Lean-Agile change that reflects Lean-Agile values and demonstrates Lean-Agile process and thinking in operation

Whilst it's hard to separate Agendashift from Lean-Agile thinking, it is very much a change management framework and engagement model rather than a delivery process, and there's nothing particularly IT-specific or development-specific about it. It has been used outside of IT, with participants as diverse as event planners, training material designers, C-suite executives, and new joiners. It has been used at organisations in industries as varied as financial services, air travel, energy supply, electronics manufacturing, and the non-profit sector.

Improvement, change, and continuous transformation

Two challenges confront the author of any book on change: the way that words like *transformation, change,* and *improvement* have become overloaded with different and sometimes contradictory interpretations, and the very different reactions that they provoke in people.

It is important to be clear from the outset that Lean and Agile both come with the strong expectation that organisations and their processes should continue to evolve. For those who object to the word *transformation* on the grounds that it necessarily implies only time-bound projects, let's for the purposes of this book agree that *transformation* here is intended as shorthand for *continuous transformation*. This I take to imply:

- Respect for the present and the past, the current context and the open-ended journey
- Appropriate ambition for the future – avoiding grandiosity but still maintaining a level of ambition greater than that typically associated with *continuous improvement, inspect and adapt,* and the like

put in slides

- Anticipation and proactivity, not just responding to pressures but shaping the future

- Self-perpetuation, change expected and sustained by the organisation's core systems

Another tricky word is *change*, and not just for the reactions it provokes. It can refer either to a very broad concept, or to a specific quantum of transformation. In the latter sense, the individual changes we refer to are often small and relatively easy to implement, but we mustn't make the mistake of allowing difficult changes to be dismissed too readily as 'unactionable'.

Finally, an *improvement* is just a change – small or large – that made things better. We're humble enough to admit that we can know this for sure only in retrospect.

Navigating Agendashift

Structure and key components

The five chapters of this book are modelled on the five main activities of our transformation strategy workshops:

1. **Discovery** – articulating something about where we are, current and future needs, and where we'd like to get to

2. **Exploration** – identifying opportunities for positive change

3. **Mapping** – visualising our plans and priorities, reviewing strategy

4. **Elaboration** – generating and framing actions, testing our thinking

5. **Operation** – learning to treat change as real work, embedding the transformation process

If those activity names have a ring of familiarity, it's because our change process is intended to mirror a Lean-Agile delivery process. This activity flow is the first of four key components.

The second component is our Lean-Agile-inspired *True North* statement:

Everyone able to work consistently at their best:

- Individuals, teams, between teams, across the organisation and beyond
- Right conversations, right people, best possible moment
- Needs anticipated, met at just the right time

We'll cover this in chapter 1 as the focus of a Discovery exercise.

The third component is the *Agendashift delivery assessment*, a distinctively non-prescriptive organisational assessment tool, typically deployed as an online survey. It makes its first appearance in chapter 2, Exploration, and resurfaces in chapter 5, Operation, in the modified form of an adaptability assessment. The six category headings of both assessments will be familiar to readers of *Kanban from the Inside*: they're the titles of its first six chapters, namely Transparency, Balance, Collaboration, Customer focus, Flow, and Leadership. Together with Understanding, Agreement, and Respect, they make up the nine values of my 2013 values model for the Kanban Method (since formally adopted into the method), in whose development I made explicit reference to Agile and Lean.

What if we removed these two consciously Lean-Agile components? Two possible answers are given in chapter 5, Operation: Agendashift interpreted as a coaching framework, and component four, the Agendashift activity flow distilled into a set of five principles for 21st century change leadership:

1. Start with needs

2. Agree on outcomes

3. Keep the agenda for change visible

4. Manage options, testing assumptions

5. Organise for clarity, speed, and mutual accountability

The four Agendashift components – the activity flow, the True North, the assessments, and the principles – feature in the poster shown in *Figure 1*, available for download at www.agendashift.com/poster. To ease your familiarisation with the activity flow you'll find highlighted excerpts of the poster at the top of each chapter.

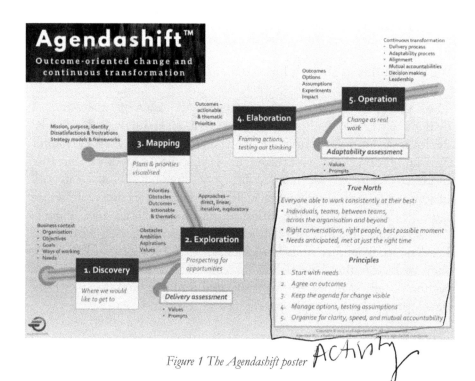

Figure 1 The Agendashift poster

Reading sequence

For a quick sample, read chapters 1 and 5. Chapter 1, Discovery, provides a practical introduction to outcome orientation; Chapter 5, Operation (a more demanding read if you've skipped the intervening chapters) develops the theme of continuous transformation.

For a slightly longer read, you can get a participant's feel for the process by reading all five chapters but skipping their respective **Behind the scenes** sections. These are always at the end of each chapter – I'm a strong believer in *"experience before explanation"*, so the exercises always come first. Of course, if you're someone who likes to understand how it all fits together, you'll want to read all five chapters from start to finish.

You'll see powerful exercises that can be used integrated or standalone, and demonstrations of tools and techniques you can use to enrich your coaching interactions. In roughly the order of their introduction, you'll see elements drawn from Clean Language, Cynefin, Agile, Lean Startup, Lean, and Kanban.

Email me at mike@agendashift.com if you have feedback of any kind. Meanwhile, if you're liking what you're reading, an appreciative tweet to hashtag #agendashift would be wonderful. Thank you.

Chapter 1. Discovery

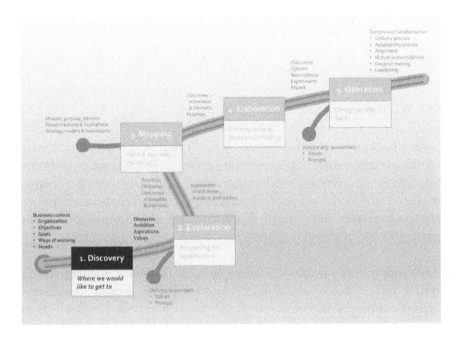

Without further ado (you did read the introduction, right?), let's begin our first exercise.

The Celebration (5W)

Picture the scene: It's some months from now, and you're celebrating! Isn't it wonderful to see everyone together like this? And you deserve it: over this period, you, your teams, and your entire organisation have achieved far more than anyone would have thought possible. You dared to aim high, and still you smashed it!

What makes this celebration so special? We're going to explore that via some time travel and the classic journalistic questions of Who, What, When, Where, and Why, otherwise known as the five W's. Get out your reporter's notepad (or a sheet of paper) and write down those headings. In our enquiries we'll start at the When and work backwards through the What and the Who before wrapping things up with the Where and the Why. (We'll address the How afterwards, in case you were wondering.)

Q: When is that celebration?

What date did you program into your time machine? How much time was needed before you had something this worthwhile to celebrate?

Q: What are you celebrating?

Looking back, what accomplishments seem the most meaningful? Start with the accomplishments that would be recognisable from outside the organisation: significant deliveries, new product developments, completed projects, service improvements, financial and customer satisfaction targets met, and so on. What made these important? What was the level of challenge involved?

After those public successes, identify accomplishments that were more internal, less visible to the outside observer. What impact (direct and indirect) did they make?

Q: Who is celebrating?

Who deserves to be there? A simple enough question, but don't stop at 'the team' or limit yourself to people we might call 'contributors'. Who helped you? Who influenced you? Who helped you simply by getting out of the way? What part did your suppliers and customers play in your successes? Whose needs did you meet?

You might find it helpful to draw or refer to pictures of some kind – for example diagrams of your process flow, charts of your organisational structure, network maps showing who influences whom, perhaps even visualisations of market structure if you need to think that big.

Who else should be there? What about people that supported you from outside your work context? Where did your energy and resilience come from?

Q: Where is that celebration?

Where are you? A cozy corner in a nice restaurant? Wembley Stadium? In a function room at your place of work? Outside at a barbecue, beer in hand, children playing?

Q: Why are you all here?

Listen to what everyone is saying as they look back on this special period. How do they describe their involvement? What motivated them? Out of all the things achieved together over these special months, what stands out as the most meaningful? In what ways has your collective success benefited each of them individually? Why does any of it matter?

The True North exercise: Everyone able to work consistently at their best

That opening exercise was more than just a chance to get to know each other. Through the conceit of the celebration and the structure of the 5W questions you have managed to share some important context and capture something of the scope and scale of the organisational challenge. It's time now to address the How.

I recall some of my career-defining accomplishments with mixed feelings. I can look back on a genuinely mission-critical project getting delivered early and there's a positive sense of pride there certainly. I have positive memories of the camaraderie, the bonds forged with colleagues in the face of struggle. But there was a dark side too: long stretches of severe pressure, relentless effort, interrupted nights, separation both physically and mentally from loved ones. These all took a toll, and not just on those that signed up to the work. Was it worth it?

That's what my How looked like a few years go. For yours, I offer two alternate realities. One requires of unsustainable levels of effort over 20-hour working days, living on pizza and heroic quantities of coffee, and sleeping under desks. Don't like that one? Let's imagine something more radical. What if your celebration-worthy accomplishments have been achieved because consistently:

- Everyone is able to work at their best – individually, within their teams, and between teams, across the organisation and beyond

- The right conversations involving the right people take place at the best possible moment

- Needs are anticipated and met at just the right time

Q: What's that like? What's different?

What *is* that like? "Fantastic!" you might say (I get that answer a lot). Digging deeper:

- What is it like for individuals to be able to work consistently at their best? What is it like for teams? Between teams, across the wider organisation? And beyond the organisation's boundaries to its users, customers, and other stakeholders?

- What is happening now that wasn't happening before? What is no longer happening? What are you seeing more of? Less of?

- What is the effect of those "right people, best possible moment" conversations? What causes them to happen?

- What is it like to have needs anticipated and those frustrating delays removed?

- What's the external impact of these changes? What would your other stakeholders (the people you previously identified that aren't the ones doing the work) make of it all? Did they help you by making changes too?

Q: What obstacles stand in the way?

Take a fresh piece of paper and write just one heading this time: **Obstacles**.

Clearly, much has changed. What obstacles did you need to overcome in order for *everyone able to work consistently at their best* to be achieved? If it helps, switch off your time machine (it's ok, you won't be needing it again) and work in the present, the here and now. What obstacles must you overcome?

When you're done, review your list. Try to phrase your obstacles so that they're not written in terms of something's absence. For example, instead of these:

- Conversations not happening until it's too late
- Slack (the messaging system) not rolled out widely enough

Focus instead on what is actually happening:

- People holding on to vital information until scheduled meetings take place or something goes wrong
- People relying on email at times when more immediate forms of communication would be more appropriate

Recasting your obstacles like this can have two important benefits. The first is that it encourages you to be specific. Specific obstacles are much easier to overcome than over-generalised ones. The second is that it helps you avoid a common trap, that of describing a problem only in terms of the absence of some prematurely-specified solution. Not only does this lazy thinking deny people the opportunity to consider or create other options, it tends to hide the full extent of underlying problems.

15-minute FOTO

In just 15 minutes, we're going go from obstacles to outcomes. It's a simple team game or coaching exercise in which you take obstacles from your list one at a time and from them generate as many desired outcomes as you can. Of course, I could just ask you to write some outcomes down, but where would be the fun in that? As in any good game there are some constraints: it's played against the clock, and there are rules.

In the full version of the game there are four player roles. It is preferable to have each role fulfilled by different people, but if you're playing solo you won't have that luxury. The responsibilities of each role are as follows:

1. **Client** ('coachee', not customer): presents obstacles and speaks for the organisation

2. **Coach**: guides the conversation

3. **Scribe**: takes notes on the conversation, listening to the client for anything that might be an outcome (however weak or vague)

4. **Observer** (optional): observes the process, monitors the conversation, intervenes if necessary

The game proceeds as a series of conversations, each initiated by the client identifying an obstacle. Each conversation then alternates between client and coach. But there's a catch: once the obstacle has been introduced, the coach is required to stick to a menu of just six *clean questions*:

1. What would you like to have happen?

2. (When X) Then what happens?

3. What is happening when X?

4. What happens before X?

5. What kind of X?

6. Is there anything else about X?

Once an obstacle is in play, the coach uses only these questions, replacing the X's with words the client has previously spoken, repeated verbatim. The questions can be used in any order and it's ok to keep repeating a question. In the demonstration below, the coach uses repetition to good effect – at the beginning to help the conversation set off in a positive direction, and later to keep it flowing whilst respecting the constraints of the game. I've underlined and numbered any words or phrases the scribe might recognise as outcomes and used italics wherever coach has substituted the client's own words for each 'X' in the question template:

Coach: What's the next obstacle on your list?

Client: Our standup meetings are rubbish!

Coach: What would you like to have happen?

Client: They take far too long

Coach: What would you LIKE to have happen?

Client: Well, shorter meetings(1) would be good

Coach: Then what happens?

Client: We'll all get back to work more quickly(2)

Coach: Then what happens?

Client: We'll be a lot more productive(3)

Coach: What kind of *productive*?

Client: The kind of productive where our time isn't wasted by conversations of no direct interest to us(4)

Coach: What kind of *conversations of no direct interest to us*?

Client: Gossip sometimes, but also problem-solving conversations

Coach: Is there anything else about *problem-solving conversations*?

Client: I'd like to see them [*problem-solving conversations*] happening as soon as the problem arises(5), but for starters we can at least keep them [*problem-solving conversations*] out of our standups(6)

Coach: What happens before we can *at least keep them out of our standups*?

Client: We'll need some working agreements on how our standups are conducted(7), with those conversations parked and rescheduled right away(8)

Coach: Then what happens?

Client: We'll have <u>more disciplined meetings</u>(9) and we should be <u>confident that issues will be dealt with properly</u>(10)

Coach: Then what happens?

Client: <u>Issues get resolved sooner</u>(11), <u>work gets delivered more quickly</u>(12), <u>happier customers</u>(13), …

I make that 13 outcomes from a single obstacle. Not bad!

What would you like to have happen?

This is the coach's question of choice near the start of each conversation. Remember that each conversation starts with an obstacle, something the client wishes wasn't there or didn't happen. "What would you like to have happen?" tends to have the effect of 'flipping' obstacles into outcomes, the client responding with something much more positive. Not always though! As in my demonstration, the coach may need to repeat this question if the client seems determined to offload multiple obstacles.

Given that the object of the game is to generate outcomes, coaches should be ready to use this question whenever necessary – mid conversation as well as at the beginning – resisting the natural temptation to explore obstacles in more detail.

(When X) Then what happens?

This question explores sequence, consequence, and impact. Given an outcome, asking this question is likely to result in another outcome. Ask it repeatedly, and you might get a whole chain of outcomes.

"Then what happens?" on its own may be all you need. You may however find it helpful to precede it with the optional "When X" part, either so that you can refer back to an earlier part of the conversation, or to encourage yourself to listen better:

And when *we'll all be a lot more productive*, **then what happens?**

Don't worry if it sounds slightly odd – it's only a game, remember!

What is happening when X?

You might be amazed at how far you can get with just the first two questions, *"What would you like to have happen?"* and *"Then what happens?"*. Before this line of questioning begins to feel too relentless however, you can pause and take stock with "What is happening when X?". Ask this question to get more context about an obstacle or outcome (it works with both), or to find out what observations might have prompted a diagnosis or judgement the client has given.

There are several points in the script above where this question could have been used. For example:

Client: They take far too long

Coach: **What is happening when** *they take far too long?*

Had the coach chosen to use this question at this early stage in the conversation, there's a good chance that the client's complaint about time-wasting conversations might have surfaced sooner. There's the risk though that the conversation turns negative and there are no outcomes to record, so use with care!

What happens before X?

Perhaps you don't understand the leap of logic that leads to the outcome you've just heard. No problem – just reel the conversation back:

What happens just before *everyone's a millionaire and we're breaking open the champagne?*

The "just" here is allowed; "immediately" would be fine too. The coach asks this question in the reasonable expectation that events occurring close together in time will be causally related somehow.

What kind of X?

Ask this very powerful question when you hear something abstract and you think it could be useful to identify something more specific:

What kind of *productive?*

What kind of *collaborative***?**

Occasionally the answer you receive to this very powerful question will be highly unexpected and very illuminating. If it feels like the conversation is moving into metaphor, don't worry – it can be a sign that an important insight is revealing itself. Go with it!

Is there anything else about X?

If *"What kind of X?"* is a clean way to ask *"Can you be more specific?"*, then *"Is there anything else about X?"* is a clean alternative to *"Can you elaborate?"*. It's also a handy way to go back and explore something that was said at some earlier point in the conversation.

Let's play

Get organised with the list of obstacles in front of the client, the menu of clean questions for the coach (see Figure 2), and paper and pen for the scribe.

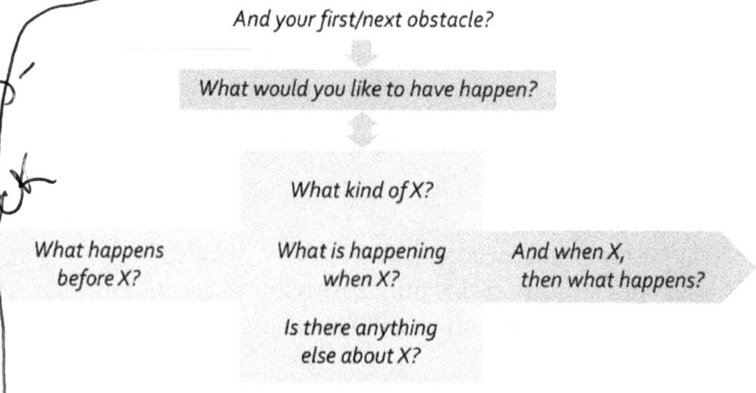

And your first/next obstacle?

What would you like to have happen?

What kind of X?

What happens before X?   What is happening when X?   And when X, then what happens?

Is there anything else about X?

Figure 2 15-minute FOTO *cue card*

20

Set a timer for 15 minutes, invite the client to start each conversation with a new obstacle, and see how many outcomes you can generate.

Tips: Don't wait for the perfectly-formed outcome. Scribe, write them all down, however weak or vague they may sound. Client, out of consideration for the scribe, keep your answers short. Coach, stick to the clean questions (scribe, it's down to you to monitor this if you don't have a separate observer). All of you (and the observer especially), don't hesitate to proceed to the next obstacle if at any time you find that you are getting bogged down. You might agree up front to rotate roles from time to time so that everyone gets a turn.

Review, revise, and organise

Take some time together to review the list of outcomes you've generated. If you have fewer than a dozen or so, try playing for a few minutes longer (in reality, 15 minutes isn't long for this game, but a sense of urgency helps), try involving more people (it isn't really a solo game), or consider getting some help. Your friendly neighbourhood coach, consultant, or facilitator should be able to pick up this exercise quickly if they're not already familiar with it.

With agreement, feel free to edit or discard any outcomes of dubious quality. Rephrase any that read like actions or solutions. If they all seem too abstract to be actionable, use the **What kind of X?** or **Is there anything else about X?** questions on the most meaningful ones to generate more for your list.

An easy way to organise your outcomes is under these three headings:

- **Short term** – urgent outcomes, action areas, immediate opportunities
- **Medium term** – intermediate objectives, signs that you're winning
- **Long term** – ambitions, goals, aspirations, values

Now you have a simple plan-on-a-page you can keep and refer back to later. Here (Figure *3*) is an example produced at a public workshop in Leeds, UK:

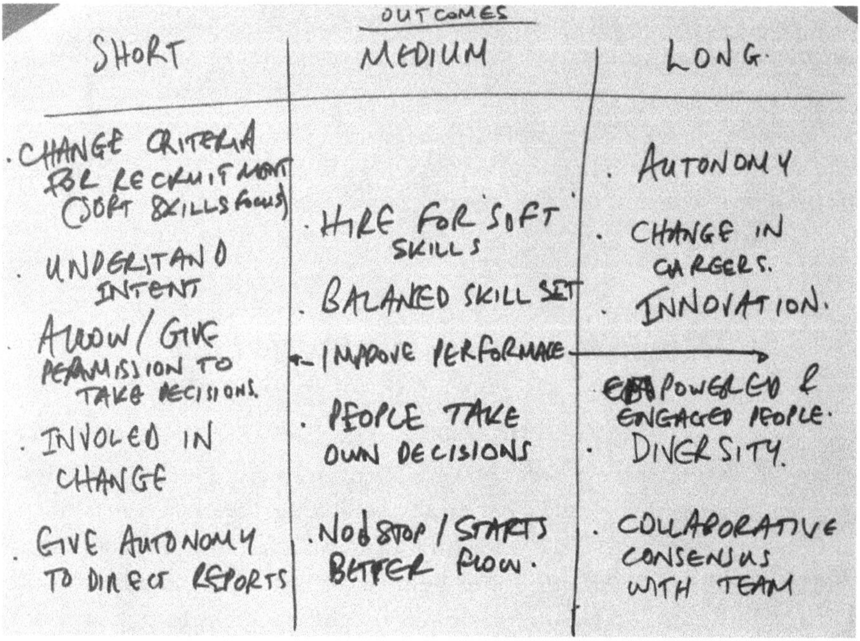

Figure 3 Outcomes, organised into a simple plan-on-a-page

You could take this further, collecting together your hopes, priorities, and rationale for your transformation. And it's only chapter 1! Don't let me stop you, but before you share such a plan, I'd recommend that you first:

1. Invite others to join you in the process, repeating the exercises of this chapter with the right people in the room

2. Find out where the true opportunities lie, obtaining sufficient detail for you to make informed judgements about scope, objectives, priorities, and approach

I leave with you the issues of invitation and participation. Seriously consider getting help from someone impartial to the specifics of your situation, experienced in the transformation process, and skilled in facilitating exercises like these. We'll address questions of detail in the next chapter, **Exploration**.

Behind the scenes

Rediscovering Discovery

The Agile manifesto (agilemanifesto.org) begins with these words:

> *"We are uncovering better ways of developing software by doing it and helping others do it."* ? for Slides

I don't know what guided the choice of the word *"uncovering"*, but *"discovering"* might have done the job equally well. It's a word that is quite familiar in Agile circles; often it's the name given to the most 'upstream' activity of the delivery process, the activity responsible for understanding customers, other stakeholders, and their different motivations for interacting with the product or service in question. From that comes a better understanding of what should be delivered.

Already we have seen that there are at least two quite distinct kinds of Discovery:

1. **Process/operational discovery**: Uncovering opportunities large and small to change how things work

2. **Product/service discovery**: Understanding the needs that products and services should fulfil, especially the needs that help to define what those products and services are for

There's a third kind of Discovery that's less widely recognised but is just as important:

3. **Organisational/strategic discovery**: Rediscovering and reaffirming what the organisation is about – its purpose, its values, the 'strategic needs' it seeks to address, how it serves society, and so on – the ultimate reference points for the organisation's alignment mechanisms

The three discovery activities help to orient process, product, and organisation (the corners of the triangle in Figure 4) towards future potential and – we hope – lasting success.

Figure 4 The Organisation/Product/Process triangle

Dysfunction arises when any of these three Discovery activities are done poorly or misalignments between them go unaddressed: the organisation lacks a sense of direction, products and services don't seem to fit, and sources of dissatisfaction and frustration seem to be everywhere. These are often attributed to a lack of leadership, but that's one of those lazy 'lack of' or 'absence' diagnoses that I wouldn't leave unchallenged even if I sympathised with it. Dig deeper! What's happening when you see lack of leadership (or lack of anything else)? Go discover!

Time travel games

There are a number of *serious games* that view the present and its unfolding choices from the reference points of one or more possible futures. Perhaps the best known in Agile circles are these:

- *Remember the future*
  Luke Hohmann (innovationgames.com and the 2006 book *Innovation Games*)
  www.innovationgames.com/remember-the-future/

- *The Future, Backwards*
  Dave Snowden (cognitive-edge.com)
  cognitive-edge.com/methods/the-future-backwards/

Of those two, the Agendashift *Celebration (5W)* exercise is more like Luke's but we love all three! In the two-day workshops that I co-facilitate with Karl Scotland, we use both ours and Dave's to good effect.

A Lean-Agile-inspired True North

Figure 5 The Agendashift True North

Agile has its manifesto; Lean has its pillars; both have their respective sets of principles. Lean-Agile has no great need of its own versions of these, but I do humbly offer the words of Figure *5* as a Lean-Agile-inspired *True North* statement. True North is a Lean concept, a statement that is intended to be both guiding and challenging over a significant period of time, even indefinitely. This one certainly won't be reached through a one-off project!

It is fitting that an outcome-oriented process should start not with a presentation but with an invitation. Some of the groups I've facilitated have found the experience of exploring *"What's that like?"* around this

25

True North to be so cathartic that they ask repeatedly for more time. It's not hard to see why:

- If you feel that you're rarely given the opportunity to work at your best, your team doesn't work well, or you're painfully aware that teams aren't working well together, it can come as a relief to be given the opportunity to imagine a different reality

- Whether you're a front line worker or a manager, conversations happening at the wrong time (or not at all) can be very frustrating

- For most of us, knowing that we're meeting needs is crucial to finding meaning in our work

If this True North needs explanation, it comes after the experience, not before. My sources:

- Progress in the direction of *"Right conversations, right people, best possible moment"* is a key sign that Agile is going well. It could be said that Agile frameworks don't guarantee this outcome but they do at least establish patterns of frequent and regular conversation, the beginning (one hopes) of true collaboration. In contrast to the Agile manifesto and principles but without contradicting them, the statement as a whole explicitly works at scales ranging from individual to corporate (and beyond) and is not tied to product or software development.

- In a similar vein, *"…met at just the right time"* is a humanised form of Lean's *Just-in-time* (JIT) principle. The mention of *needs* is deliberate – a door-opener to the reminder that ticking off requirements, delivering solutions, and solving problems in no way guarantees that needs will be met.

- My inspiration for the phrase *"work consistently at their best"* is Caitlin Walker's *From Contempt to Curiosity: Creating the Conditions for Groups to Collaborate Using Clean Language and Systemic Modelling.* This powerful book is listed among my key Clean Language references (next section).

To enable its wider use and to encourage adaptations we've released the True North under a Creative Commons with-attribution license. Go to www.agendashift.com/true-north for details.

Clean questions and Clean Language

What a lot of questions! With rare exceptions my questions shared these characteristics:

- They weren't *binary*, but *open*. In other words, I asked questions that didn't invite a yes/no answer.

- They weren't leading questions, but *genuine* – genuine in the sense that I didn't already have a particular answer in mind.

Clean questions take this up a notch or two. The six we used in the game are just a small subset of the questions maintained by the *Clean Language* community, a community built around the work of consulting psychologist the late David Grove. For the purposes of this book I chose questions most suited to exploring outcomes; other questions can be used to explore time and space, relationships between things, and metaphor.

The questions are 'clean' in the sense that they are stripped of assumptions, promoting a state of genuine enquiry on the part of the coach. Once you start to practice Clean Language, you heighten your self-awareness, noticing when you're judging or advising before you've properly listened. If you have any interest at all in coaching, I wholeheartedly recommend that you explore it further.

My own experience of Clean Language started with these three books, in this order:

- *The Five Minute Coach: Improve Performance Rapidly*
Lynne Cooper & Mariette Castellino (2012, Crown House Publishing)

- *Clean Language: Revealing Metaphors and Opening Minds*
Wendy Sullivan & Judy Rees (2008, Crown House Publishing)

- *From Contempt to Curiosity: Creating the Conditions for Groups to Collaborate Using Clean Language and Systemic Modelling*
  Caitlin Walker (2014, Clean Publishing)

Also this helpful paper by Penny Tomkins and James Lawley, describing the PRO (problem-remedy-outcomes) model from a Clean Language perspective:

- *Coaching for P.R.O.'s*
  Tomkins & Lawley (2006, cleanlanguage.co.uk)
  www.cleanlanguage.co.uk/articles/articles/31/1/Coaching-for-PROs/Page1.html

Via www.agendashift.com/resources you can obtain:

1. Artwork for the cue card shown in *Figure 2*. I recommend that you get a generous supply of these printed on A5-sized card, enough that you can let participants keep theirs after playing the game. I get them printed by the hundred!

2. A deck for facilitators

Note that the cards include a seventh clean question not covered in this chapter:

- Is there a relationship between X and Y?

We'll introduce this question properly in the next chapter.

What's your contract?

To finish chapter 1, another contribution from Caitlin Walker, the question *"What's your contract?"*. This question is the answer to another question, and it's an important one: When is it safe and/or sensible to use the Clean Language questions and similar coaching questions?

You need to be clear about what's expected, acceptable, and respectful to all participants when (for example):

- You're in a game whose rules and roles are familiar to all participants
- You're interviewing someone, for fact-finding reasons, for example
- You're coaching individuals, teams, or whole organisations
- You're a therapist (a real one)
- You're in an everyday situation, at work or at home

Not only is each of these situations different, what's acceptable will vary also according the people involved and your contract (explicit or implied) with them. If you're unsure, you might start with exploring the nature of that relationship.

Meanwhile, as your experience with Clean Language grows through practice in appropriate settings, so will your awareness of unhelpful patterns of questioning, your own most importantly. I've never found that kind of self-awareness something to regret, and mistakes are easily remedied if caught quickly.

Key points – 1. Discovery

Outputs:

- Context, captured through the 5W questions (Who, What, When, Where, Why) of the Celebration exercise
- Obstacles, collected after reflection and discussion around the Agendashift True North statement
- Outcomes, generated from those obstacles using the 15-minute FOTO game

Concepts and tools:

- The Agendashift True North:

    o Integrating Lean and Agile values in a statement designed to challenge and to guide

    o An invitation to consider a more positive, needs-centric How – what that's like, and what obstacles stand in the way

- 15-minute FOTO

    o From Obstacles to Outcomes in 15 minutes (or a little longer)

    o In this chapter this coaching game is used to generate outcomes from a list of specific obstacles standing in our path towards True North

    o Uses questions drawn from *Clean Language*

- Clean Language

    o Rooted in the work of consulting psychologist the late David Grove

    o Introduced here as a coaching discipline

    o 'Clean questions': open questions that are stripped of the coach's assumptions, used with the client's own words

- Three kinds of Discovery:

    1. Process/operational: Uncovering opportunities large and small to change how things work

    2. Product/service: Understanding the needs that products and services should fulfil

    3. Organisational/strategic: Rediscovering and reaffirming what the organisation is about

Chapter 2. Exploration

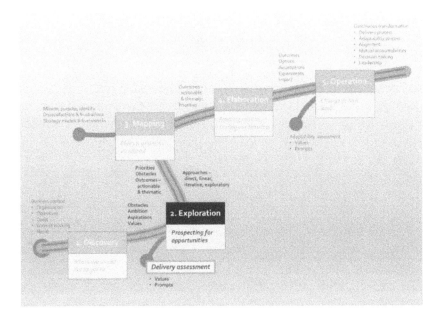

You've identified some key goals and other outcomes that will help us maintain our bearings. Soon it will be time to start work on a plan in the form of a *Transformation Map*, but before you get started on that, you'll want to get a better understanding of the landscape in which you will be operating. This is Exploration: prospecting for opportunities and preparing for Mapping.

In this chapter we will look at:

- The Agendashift delivery assessment, mini edition
- Debriefing a survey
- Prioritising areas of attention
- Generating outcomes
- Organising outcomes by approach
- Agreeing scope

In the spirit of *experience before explanation* we'll dive right in. Towards the end of the chapter we'll go behind the scenes and reveal some of the history and rationale behind the tools.

The Agendashift delivery assessment, mini edition

Here we're using a shortened version (the 'mini edition') of the *Agendashift delivery assessment*, a template for an assessment or survey that's usually done online. The full 'original edition' has a total of 43 *prompts* (they're statements, not questions); the mini edition has just 18, three for each of its six categories.

Both editions use the same 4-point scale:

1. Barely started - little evidence, if any

2. Early gains - sporadic evidence, not widespread or consistent

3. Getting there - evident, but improvement or more consistency needed

4. Nailing it, consistently - firmly established, widely and consistently evident

The scale is designed such that you'll easily recognise if you're a 1 or 4. There is no lazy middle option if you're at neither extreme; choose 2 or 3 according to whether you believe that you're closer to the beginning or the end of your journey.

Category 1: Transparency

The first three prompts are presented without explanation. It would be no different even if we were sat together: I'd be listening more than talking, noting down any interesting comments as you work your way through them.

1.1   Our delivery process and the work items currently in progress within it are easily visible to all involved and interested parties

1.2   We have visibility of work items due to enter the delivery process soon

1.3   We can see which work items are blocked and for what reason

On our 1-4 scale, what scores would you give to each of these prompts?

Before you move on to the next category, pause for a moment. Which (if any) of the prompts are you drawn to? Why do they resonate with you?

Category 2: Balance

In the same manner – using the same scoring scale and taking the same pause at the end – use the prompts of the **Balance** category:

2.1   We bring work into the delivery process only as capacity allows, preferring to finish work items already in progress than to start new work items

2.2   We maintain a clear separation between work currently in progress and work still under consideration

2.3   We take steps to avoid being overburdened with more work-in-progress than we can accommodate effectively

Now continue with categories 3-6, namely Collaboration, Customer focus, Flow, and Leadership.

Category 3: Collaboration

3.1   We work with those whose needs we are meeting in order to understand, shape and size potential work before committing to deliver it

3.2   Our delivery process encourages collaboration across roles and specialties

3.3   We meet on a regular basis to review and improve our outputs and processes

Category 4: Customer Focus

4.1   We seek to align our work to shared goals, prioritising for maximum impact

4.2   We incorporate customer feedback into our work while it is in the delivery process

4.3   We continue to own work items until the customer confirms that their needs are being met

Category 5: Flow

5.1   We can predict with reasonable confidence how long it will take to deliver work of typical value and risk

5.2   We understand the performance of our delivery system in sufficient detail to make timely decisions, to set appropriate expectations, and to focus our improvement efforts

5.3   We proactively identify and address dependencies and other impediments to flow

Category 6: Leadership

6.1   Together, we strive to meet customer needs, improve our delivery systems, and develop new capabilities; in all three pursuits we are appropriately recognised, supported, and rewarded

6.2   We ensure that opportunities for improvement are recognised and systematically followed through

6.3   We all share the responsibility to seek clarification, to highlight problems, and to come up with improvement ideas

Review

Now quickly review your scores – all 18, across the 6 categories. Does the overall distribution seem to make sense? What's your most common score?

And review the prompts themselves, reminding yourself of the those you were most drawn to as you paused at the end of each category. Across the assessment as a whole, what would be your top 5? Top 3? Top 1?

It should now be apparent that scoring the prompts is just a prelude to the main event. Although the scores may have some interest in themselves, the scoring exercise really serves to encourage you to think more carefully about these things:

- What the prompts mean, and perhaps the intention behind them
- How well they describe your current context
- How they might apply differently in some future context
- Which prompts are important right now, and why

Debriefing a survey

Now for a slight change in perspective. From capturing one person's assessment (yours), we'll jump forward to debriefing a survey that consolidates the inputs of multiple participants. The survey in question might have been conducted through face-to-face sessions, in a workshop setting, entirely online without coaching support, or some combination. The mechanics will vary, but two general principles apply:

- Answers may vary according to the organisational scope of the exercise – participants often score their own teams higher than they would the wider organisation – so it's a good idea to discuss scope with your sponsors ahead of time and to communicate this clearly to participants before they start.

- The debrief session should be as inclusive as possible, representative of those who will be impacted by any change that is likely to result. This may mean conducting multiple debriefs and circling round afterwards to form some overall view.

We recommend the following structure to the debrief:

- Score distributions
- Strongest and weakest
- Areas of apparent agreement and disagreement

This structure is now so well established that we've made the online reporting tools support it explicitly.

Score distributions

These histograms (Figure 6) show the overall distribution of scores given in the survey.

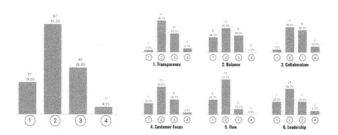

Figure 6 Summary histograms

I would make the following observations about this particular example:

- The *mode* (the most common score) here is 2 (*early gains*) – both overall and in every category
- There are more 1's and 2's (*barely started* and *early gains*) than 3's and 4's (*getting there* and *nailing it, consistently*); the *median* (middle) score is also 2

Do these statistics imply that things are especially bad here? Probably not. Surveys with a mode of 3 aren't rare, but a mode of 2 is significantly more common. In this situation I would give the reassurance that I see this often, they're in good company, and that two years of global surveys have generated very similar results. Any feelings of disappointment can be directed at the state of our industry; we meanwhile have work to do!

Strongest and weakest

Naturally, people are often keen to know where the scores come out stronger or weaker. Here (Figure 7) are the histograms again, this time sorted strongest category first:

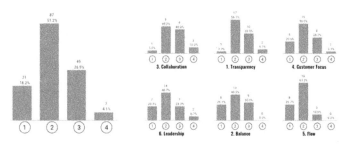

Figure 7 Summary histograms, sorted strongest first

With this example data in front of us, my briefest of debriefs would consist mainly of just two questions to the room:

1. "Collaboration first, then Transparency and Customer Focus: your thoughts on those as your strongest categories?"

2. "Something has to come out weakest, and here it seems to be Leadership, Balance, and – weakest of all – Flow. Thoughts?"

Then a third and much harder question:

3. "I'm fascinated that two of these categories have ended up together. Can you guess which I'm referring to?"

Very much a 'quiz question' that last one, not intended as an example of great facilitation. It doesn't happen every time, but very often you'll notice a strong correlation between Balance and Flow. It's not surprising: would you expect good flow if you don't keep your workload under control? Overburdened systems – systems whose workloads are out of balance with their capacity – don't perform well. Neither do systems that have parts starved of good quality work.

Time permitting, we might review the strongest few prompts of the strongest few categories, and the weakest few prompts of the weakest few categories. I don't like to spend much time on this however, and often I skip this step altogether. To understand why, let's take a look at Leadership, one of the weaker categories in this survey (Figure 8):

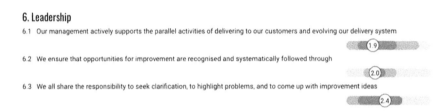

6. Leadership

6.1 Our management actively supports the parallel activities of delivering to our customers and evolving our delivery system

1.9

6.2 We ensure that opportunities for improvement are recognised and systematically followed through

2.0

6.3 We all share the responsibility to seek clarification, to highlight problems, and to come up with improvement ideas

2.4

Figure 8 A weak category

Observe how the outer of the two 'spread' bars on the first of those prompts fills most of the available width. Towards the end of this chapter comes a technical description of how these bars work; for the moment it's enough to know that we can infer two important facts:

- At least a quarter of the scores here were 1's
- Some of the scores were 4's, right at the other end of the scale

Clearly, there are some very different perceptions captured in this data! The wide range revealed here is far more interesting than any single score and our time is much better spent exploring these areas of divergence.

Agreement and disagreement

This is the meaty part of the debrief and it's an exploration of the categories and prompts that show:

1. a narrow spread of scores, especially in areas already identified as particularly weak or strong

2. a wide spread of scores, the more interesting part

Looking at the example category-level data sorted for narrowness of spread (Figure 9), I would make the observation that the data suggests agreement on the relative strength of Transparency and the relative weakness of Flow.

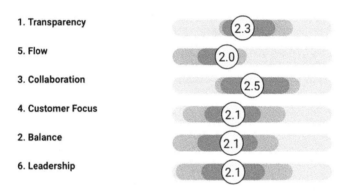

1. Transparency   2.3

5. Flow   2.0

3. Collaboration   2.5

4. Customer Focus   2.1

2. Balance   2.1

6. Leadership   2.1

Figure 9 Narrowest (most agreement) first

The prompt-level data for Flow confirms the suspicion (Figure 10):

5.1 We can predict with reasonable confidence how long it will take to deliver work of typical value and risk

(2.0)

5.2 We understand the performance of our delivery system in sufficient detail to make timely decisions, to set appropriate expectations, and to focus our improvement efforts

(1.5)

5.3 We proactively identify and address dependencies and other impediments to flow

(2.0)

Figure 10 Prompt-level data for Flow

A narrow range of answers, for prompt 5.3 especially.

Much more interesting are the areas of apparent disagreement (Figure *11*). Note the slight change of format: I've removed the section headings, showing a 'tagged' view instead:

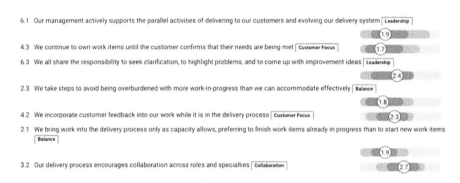

6.1 Our management actively supports the parallel activities of delivering to our customers and evolving our delivery system [Leadership]

(1.9)

4.3 We continue to own work items until the customer confirms that their needs are being met [Customer Focus]

(1.7)

6.3 We all share the responsibility to seek clarification, to highlight problems, and to come up with improvement ideas [Leadership]

(2.4)

2.3 We take steps to avoid being overburdened with more work-in-progress than we can accommodate effectively [Balance]

(1.8)

4.2 We incorporate customer feedback into our work while it is in the delivery process [Customer Focus]

(2.3)

2.1 We bring work into the delivery process only as capacity allows, preferring to finish work items already in progress than to start new work items [Balance]

(1.9)

3.2 Our delivery process encourages collaboration across roles and specialties [Collaboration]

(2.7)

Figure 11 Widest spread (apparent disagreement) first

I am now happy to spend as much time as we need discussing these results line by line, probing with question such as these:

- "Who scored a 3 or 4 for this one and wouldn't mind sharing their thinking?"
- "Who has good examples of this working well?"
- "Who's different to that? Who had a 1 or a 2?"
- "What's the impact when it's not working well?"
- "What do you think drives this behaviour?"

If you think it that the conversation will flow more freely if a sense of anonymity is retained, you can begin with:

- "Who can imagine why someone might score a 3 or a 4 here?"

- "What might explain the 1's and 2's?"

The reasons for disagreement on scores can be perfectly legitimate:

- Differences in understanding of the scope of the exercise (typically, the more limited the scope the higher the score)

- Different specific examples (good or bad) sticking in the memory

- Differences in understanding of what the prompts mean

- Differences in understanding of what's possible (and therefore what a 4 looks like)

The good news is that none of these differences undermine the process. The goal isn't to arrive at a single agreed score but to build a shared sense of how really things are. Through shared stories – 'micro-narratives' if you like – we build a platform for later agreement on where the opportunities lie and what's to be done.

Quick recap

An overview of the debrief so far:

- Overall and per-category score distributions, mode and median

- Stronger and weaker categories, perhaps a few of the strongest and weakest prompts in the stronger and weaker categories

- Narrowest spread – consistency within categories and agreement on scores at prompt level

- Widest spread – wide ranges of scores within categories and at prompt level, areas of apparent disagreement for more in-depth discussion

Agreement on action areas

Prioritising areas of attention

Cast your mind back to those moments of reflection after the completion of your assessment. You were asked to identify your top 5, top 3, and top 1 prompts. In a workshop setting this is best done in table groups of four to six people:

- Working silently, each participant chooses their personal top 3 prompts
- Working in pairs or threes, their top 5
- Table groups then agree their top 5

Printed handouts are invaluable; a couple per table group should suffice (the online tools make this easy).

We'll allow a few minutes for this before hearing from each table group in turn. Groups will have some choices in common and some differences; it's not important that they're in close agreement, only that they have been heard.

Generating and organising outcomes

So far we have facilitated agreement on how things are and where the opportunities lie. Now comes the generative part, generating outcomes using a process similar to that described in chapter 1:

- Review the selected prompts in priority order, discussing and writing down a list of obstacles that stand in their way

- Flip these obstacles into outcomes using the clean questions (Figure *12*) of the 15-minute FOTO game (Chapter 1):

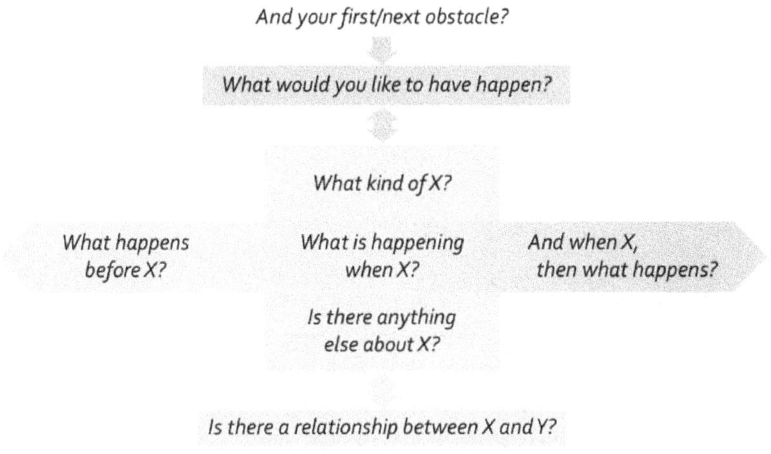

And your first/next obstacle?

What would you like to have happen?

What kind of X?

What happens before X?	*What is happening when X?*	*And when X, then what happens?*

Is there anything else about X?

Is there a relationship between X and Y?

Figure 12 15-minute FOTO cue card

It's a good idea to record against each obstacle and outcome the ID number of the prompt to which it belongs – it may save you some time later.

You may find that obstacles get flipped into solution ideas with no outcome explicitly identified. 'Scribes' in this situation should write these down but 'coaches' please don't stop there. Ask *"Then what happens?"* and let the process continue.

Typically, you will find that when you ask *"Then what happens?"* several times you will generate a chain of outcomes that become increasingly abstract. Be ready to stop this line of questioning before it gets too repetitive or circular but do persist until then – you might be identifying important themes. As you reach this point, the question *"What kind of X?"* can be especially thought-provoking. It invites the 'client' to imagine – perhaps for the first time – what these more thematic outcomes might come to mean for them.

Aside: Circular conversations may feel frustrating at the time, but they can be an indication of something interesting. They might be uncovering a potential virtuous circle or a hidden feedback loop of some other kind. More on these in Chapter 5.

Is there a relationship between X and Y?

You'll have noticed that the cue card has gained a seventh clean question:

- Is there a relationship between X and Y?

We avoided this question in chapter 1, and with good reason: it's easy to use this question in a way that's well outside Clean Language's good intentions, so we recommend that you don't use it until you've had some practice with the more basic questions. The risk with this question is that instead of helping the client to explore their landscape of goals, obstacles, and outcomes, the coach starts to offer judgements and diagnoses of their own. For example:

- Is there a relationship between your weight and your love of chocolate?

Whatever your thoughts on the appropriateness of such a question, now is definitely not the time. Here, use this clean question only if it's 100% genuine – in other words when you don't already have the answer yourself.

In particular, it may be helpful to use this question to explore carefully the relationships between the outcomes being generated in Exploration and goals already articulated during Discovery. As the coach, you might be motivated by a worry that the client may be heading towards a dead end, an outcome that brings their goals no closer to fruition. However, you must also be open to the possibility that the client possesses some key insight that you haven't yet uncovered. Keeping the questioning clean is a good way for both of you to find out which of those possibilities is indeed the right one.

Organise your outcomes with the Four Points exercise

With 15 or more outcomes to play with, this next exercise can be very instructive. We're going to organise the outcomes, but instead of doing it by theme (*affinity clustering*, as the technique is known), we're going to do it in a way that can be remarkably revealing about individual and corporate attitudes to change.

You will need:

- Your outcomes transferred onto sticky notes (one outcome per sticky, each labelled with their respective prompt ID's) and laid out in front of you so that you can read them all

- A convenient square of wall that's at least four times the area currently occupied by your stickies, so that they will have room to move as you organise them

Bottom right

We're going to start at the bottom right hand corner of your square. Taking as much time as you need, carefully choose from your list the strongest single example of an outcome where ***there's an approach you can all see and agree on***. In other words, you can straightforwardly agree how your outcome can be realised with reasonable certainty. You may not feel that this describes any of your outcomes especially well, but that's ok – choose your best one, and place it tightly into the bottom right hand corner (Figure 13).

Figure 13 Bottom right corner

Top right

Next, the top right corner (Figure 14). Select the strongest single example of an outcome where **an expert or some research will determine a good approach**. Here you believe that some degree of expertise is both necessary and sufficient; it is reasonable to expect this outcome to be susceptible to the kind of analysis that will deliver a reliable plan, with few unforeseen issues encountered in implementation.

Figure 14 Top right corner

Top left

Continuing anti-clockwise to the top left corner (Figure 15), carefully choose the strongest single example of an outcome where ***there's no one right approach – experts will disagree***. Not only will 10 experts give you 20 different ideas, typical of this kind of outcome is the sense that no idea is sure to get you the whole way to your outcome. Much as you might wish it to be otherwise, you couldn't just delegate this outcome to an expert and reasonably expect the whole journey to be planned for you in advance.

Figure 15 Top Left Corner

Bottom left

For the fourth and final corner of your square (Figure 16), you're looking for the strongest single example of an outcome where ***no known approach is immediately apparent***. You're not sure that an expert will help you in the time available, you don't know which of your ideas will stick, you don't know how things will settle down after they have been disrupted – whether the source of disruption is accidental or deliberate, internal or external. Tricky!

Figure 16 Bottom left corner

Your next sticky…

Now choose another sticky at random. Imagine it being drawn towards the corner stickies it is most similar to in terms of approach. It might end up next to one of them, between two, or somewhere towards the middle, drawn in various degrees towards three or four corners (Figure 17).

Figure 17 Placing sticky number five

If you decide that you can't place this sticky authentically this way, just leave it in the centre of the square.

…And the next one

Do the same with your next sticky (Figure 18), except that you're now placing it not only relative to the four corner stickies, but also relative to the fifth sticky you added just now. You might need to shuffle both of them around before it feels right.

Figure 18 Placing sticky number six

Your remaining stickies

Now add your remaining stickies one at a time, trying to place them relative to those you've placed already, rearranging as necessary. Some will have a strong affinity approach-wise with one of your four exemplars and will be easy to place near one of the corners. Others will seem to have a natural position somewhere relative to two or three existing stickies. Any that really won't be placed authentically this way should be arranged in a central region.

After you've placed all your stickies, you'll end up with something like this (Figure 19):

Figure 19 A finished Four Points exercise

In this very typical example, we have the expected clusters around the corners, a cluster midway between the two right hand corners, and the suggestion of another cluster top middle. There's one solitary sticky placed near the centre, and a few more that seem to be pulled in that direction.

Name those corners

You can now give names to your exemplar stickies (we deliberately refrained from doing this earlier, as to do so completely changes the nature of this exercise). Anticlockwise from bottom right, let's call them your 'most obvious' outcome, your 'most complicated' outcome, your 'most complex' outcome, and your 'most chaotic' outcome. Similar names can be applied to their neighbouring regions (or *domains*, as they're known): *obvious*, *complicated*, *complex*, and *chaos*. The fifth, central region has a name too: *disorder*.

The "Obvious" question

When I'm debriefing this exercise, there's a slightly tongue-in-cheek question I like to ask immediately after naming the corners:

What's the obvious question to ask about the items in the Obvious corner?

The answer I'm looking for (and always get, one way or another):

Why haven't they been done already?

After the teasing comes a serious point that has become a recurring theme for many of my workshops and longer engagements: Too many organisations are full of smart people who can tell you what's wrong and can give you a long list of sure-fire fixes, but nothing changes.

You might say that these organisations are uninterested in improvement, but I believe that in many cases it would be more constructive to say that they are incapable of following through. Some of the tell-tale signs:

- Little to no visibility or accountability around anything change-related
- The mechanisms (whether formal or informal) that do exist to track organisational initiatives are constantly overwhelmed with urgent delivery-related issues

- Little provision for understanding and tracking improvements to the systems that continue to cause those issues to arise in the first place

If these things are true even for the Obvious corner, how will those organisations achieve outcomes that require more sophisticated approaches? Not well. We'll return to these issues in Chapter 5, Operation.

Comfort zones

Now review the top half of the board, the half that contains your 'most complicated' and 'most complex' items. Do you feel drawn to one side or the other? Are you more comfortable with work that can be analysed and planned up front, or do you prefer work that is better suited to a more exploratory approach? Speaking for myself, I will rarely be accused of over-planning, and I will admit that I can spend far too long exploring my way to outcomes that could have been reached much more directly had I applied some proper forethought.

Whole organisations can show strong biases to one side or the other and the costs can be enormous. Some that I've worked with will take many months or even years planning and executing large projects even when it is known from the outset that the certainty of outcome (not to be confused with the certainty of executing the project plan) is very low. They have convinced themselves that their meticulous approach reduces risk, when to the outside observer the opposite might be argued! Over time, this bias becomes so ingrained that few people would think to challenge it. For these organisations, it's "doing it properly" or "just how we do things" – part of their culture, in other words.

Not that organisations biased towards the complex aren't prone to some serious problems of their own. It isn't just wasteful to take a trial-and-error approach when a direct route is available: it can get much worse than that. What about failing to do the due diligence? A good example is the team that explores its way to a beautiful product, only for the launch to fail spectacularly for reasons of technical flaws, operational capacity, or legal questions. Sometimes these projects blow up so spectacularly that the press takes notice. Occasionally, the consequences are devastating, with damage not just to personal and corporate reputations but to the wellbeing of customers and the wider public too.

There are some important clues here about how to avoid these failures:

1. As any competent project manager will tell you, most large endeavours are based on assumptions that must be tested before positive outcomes can be assured. Find ways to identify and test them early, ideally in ways that bring some positive benefits of their own.

2. Conversely, be prepared for some rigorous development before the full value can be realised from the results of small-scale experimentation. Avoid the trap of thinking that experimentation is enough; execution still matters.

But it doesn't stop at delivery. Even after successful execution, there still remains the vital task of validation and insight gathering. A perfect launch does not guarantee good reception; a product, service, or business initiative that isn't meeting needs still has work to do. It might be a bitter pill for some to swallow, but it must be admitted that there are few initiatives that wouldn't benefit from being thought of and managed as experiments.

Taking these together, many of your more interesting outcomes (including the outcomes you found difficult to place authentically in that last exercise) will contain aspects similar both to your 'most complicated' and to your 'most complex' outcomes. Draw out these different aspects and manage each of them appropriately.

The Chaos corner

One thing's for sure about the chaos corner: it definitely isn't intended to represent a comfort zone. Do real firefighters spend most of their time fighting fires? Of course they don't. However, you might be forgiven for thinking that this is normal, given the fondness of some organisations to keep shaking things up, to make changes without a coherent rationale, or to make only symptomatic fixes that provide no lasting relief.

There is such a thing as too little chaos, however. Organisations can get complacent; better some internal disruption before they are overwhelmed by disruption from outside. Better to innovate and risk obsoleting your own products than to have this done to you. And don't think that your little corner of your organisation is immune from competition: even internal services can be outsourced.

In cases of genuine emergency, symptomatic fixes and directive management styles might be completely justified. It may well be the case that doing nothing is not a viable option, even if the underlying truth of the situation is not yet clear to everyone (or indeed, to anyone).

Tip: In the next chapter, Mapping, we'll be creating another visualisation, the *Transformation Map*, before returning in Chapter 4, Elaboration, to the idea of different approaches to change. If you're working through these exercises over a short period – a day or two – there's the opportunity to reuse your stickies. You can save yourself a little work later if you clearly mark those sitting top left in the complex domain before you take them down. A simple asterisk will do.

Agreement on scope

A good way wrap up Exploration is to revisit and if necessary revise the plan-on-a-page that you produced in the last exercise of chapter 1, Discovery. Revising it as necessary:

- Are you still happy with the short term, medium term, and long term outcomes you identified previously? Are you clear about their organisational scope?

- Have you explored the most important themes in sufficient detail?

- Have you captured an appropriate level of ambition? Without straying into grandiosity, does your plan address key needs and provide some meaningfully stretching goals?

- Can you identify some next steps: obvious quick wins, work to be delegated, priorities for experimentation, perhaps some urgent interventions?

Behind the scenes

The assessment

Three months before the publication of *Kanban from the Inside* in the autumn of 2014, I shared an Excel-based assessment tool based on a bulleted list of recommendations I was about to include in the book's final chapter, organised by value (Transparency, Balance, Collaboration, etc). During the European conference season shortly after publication, Matt Philip came over from the US to share his positive experiences using the tool at his company. It seemed that we were on to something!

Back then, the tool was still very rough around the edges. Language that seemed perfectly fine inside the book didn't work quite so well outside of it, and these days it's just unforgiveable to distribute assessments in the form of emailed spreadsheets! I set to work on improving the prompts and putting it online.

Despite its flaws, Dragan Jojic – who was leading Radtac's culture practice at the time – was finding the tool useful and we collaborated on several iterations of improvements to the wording. Although with the benefit of hindsight it now seems obvious, we were at the time surprised to discover just how important it was to purge the wording of jargon and prescription. Eventually we settled on the style that has the prompts written as descriptive statements in the present tense, most of them starting with the inclusive "We..." or "Our...".

Testing it in the field, we found that jargon that seemed innocuous to us was capable of generating significant head-scratching. A great example is *pull*, a word that has a specific meaning to anyone who has a working knowledge of Lean. Phrases like *"pulling work into the system"* sounded natural enough to us, but not to everyone!

Even more important was the removal of practice-based prescriptions and their replacement with descriptions of outcomes. The reaction when we got this wrong was along the lines of *"We tried standup meetings and they didn't work"*, and *"Don't talk to me about metrics, they're evil"*. In a word: *resistance*. If you've ever been at the receiving end of a practice-based assessment, you may well have felt this resistance yourself, perhaps some cynicism too. Why then are consultants and their sponsors so quick to reach for prescriptive tools? Laziness is one possible explanation – getting it right is hard work!

The 18-prompt mini assessment was Patrick Steyaert's idea. Just for the record, I should note that the text of prompt 3.3 no longer appears in the full version of the assessment – in the larger 'original edition', improvements to other prompts not included in the mini edition have rendered this one redundant. Later came translations into French (Olivier My), German (Markus Hippeli and Susanne Bartel), Italian (Marco Bresciani), Russian (Nikita Vishnevskiy), Dutch (Martien van Steenbergen), Spanish (Teodora Bozheva), Hebrew (Yaki Koren), and Swedish (Johan Nordin). We continue to improve the wording, now as a community effort, with a Slack channel (#assessments on agendashift.slack.com) devoted to it.

For information about accessing the assessment online, refer to the Resources section at the back of this book.

The 'sliders'

'Slider' is the name we give to the visualisation below (Figure *20*), with its coloured and grey bars of varying widths. Typically it's enough to describe them as "just a measure of spread" but a proper description of the underlying calculations is sometimes required.

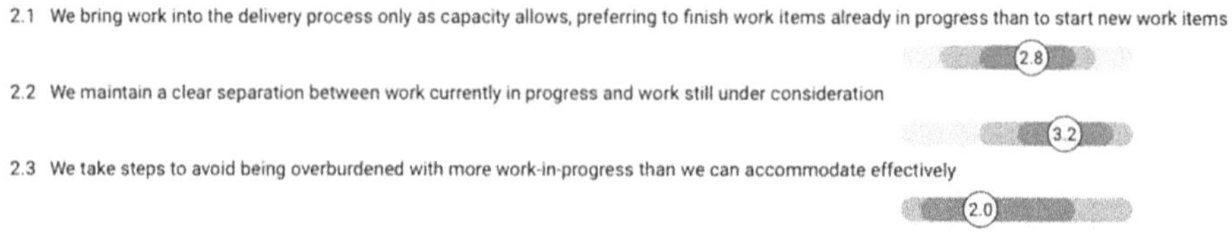

2.1 We bring work into the delivery process only as capacity allows, preferring to finish work items already in progress than to start new work items

2.8

2.2 We maintain a clear separation between work currently in progress and work still under consideration

3.2

2.3 We take steps to avoid being overburdened with more work-in-progress than we can accommodate effectively

2.0

Figure 20 'Sliders'

58

Each of the scores – 2.8, 3.2, and 2.0 in this example – is an *interquartile mean*. To calculate one of these, we take all the relevant scores, sort them, discard the top and bottom quartiles (thereby removing any outliers), and calculate the mean of the remaining data points. Statisticians describe the interquartile mean as a *robust* statistic, one that is not easily influenced by errors.

Looking at prompt 2.1 in the picture, we can say informally that the "average of the middle half" of the scores given to this prompt is 2.8 (on a scale of 1 to 4). It would be reasonable to guess that the majority of answers lie between 2 and 3, with more 3's than 2's. Not "nailing it" yet, but "getting there".

The calculations for the bars are very similar, but here we do want to be influenced by the extremes. The left and right ends of the outer bars show the means of the bottom and top quartiles respectively, the most extreme answers at the low and high ends of the scale. Notice that for prompt 2.2 this bar extends all the way to the right, and for prompt 2.3, all the way to the left. At a glance, we know that at least a quarter of the scores for prompt 2.2 must be 4's (since their mean is 4, and there can be no scores higher than 4). Similarly, at least a quarter of the scores for prompt 2.3 must be 1's.

The inner bars are also influenced by extremes, but moderated by more typical scores. The left and right ends here show the means of the bottom and top halves respectively. Looking again at prompts 2.2 and 2.3, we know that between quarter and half of the scores here were 4's and 1's respectively. Informally, "getting on for half" would be a fair description.

1-2-4-All

1-2-4-All is the name for this group facilitation pattern:

- **1**: People work silently on their own, generating ideas, making choices, or doing whatever else the exercise calls for
- **2**: People join into pairs, combining their individual results
- **4**: Pairs join up into table groups (4 people ideally) to prepare results for sharing

- **All**: The facilitator invites the table groups to share their results to the room

It's a great way to ensure that everyone gets the chance to contribute. You can find a more detailed description of this pattern on the Liberating Structures website (www.liberatingstructures.com):

- *1-2-4-All: Engage Everyone Simultaneously in Generating Questions, Ideas, and Suggestions*
  Keith McCandless & Henri Lipmanowicz
  www.liberatingstructures.com/1-1-2-4-all/

There's a book too:

- *The Surprising Power of Liberating Structures: Simple Rules to Unleash A Culture of Innovation*
  Keith McCandless & Henri Lipmanowicz
  (2014, Liberating Structures Press)

The Four Points exercise and Cynefin

The four corners of this exercise – the *Cynefin Four Points Contextualisation Exercise* to give it its full name – are pointers to the four main *domains* of Dave Snowden's Cynefin framework (Figure *21*). Dave is founder and chief scientific officer at Cognitive Edge, and his work occupies a very interesting intersection between *complexity science* (the study of complex systems) and *narrative enquiry* (a more qualitative approach, based on the capture of and thoughtful interaction with fragmented material).

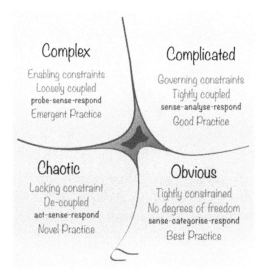

Figure 21 The Cynefin framework (source: Wikipedia)

My delay in the naming the domains (*obvious, complicated, complex, chaos,* and *disorder*) was very deliberate. Once the corners or regions are named, the temptation is to divide the square into quadrants and then just to categorise each outcome. This causes the exercise to lose much of its essential character as a *sensemaking* exercise, one in which participants interact thoughtfully with their outcomes, exploring similarities and differences between them, and waiting to see what structures might emerge. And when drawn as quadrants, the model loses Cynefin's fifth domain, the domain of *disorder*, the home of those otherwise unplaceable outcomes.

Ignoring Cynefin's sensemaking power and instead treating it as a model for casual categorisation has another quite unfortunate consequence: a perverse pride in comfort zones. "Our methods are for the complex domain" might sound impressive, but it's evidence of both of weak thinking (*Appeal to authority*) and of narrow applicability, an unwillingness to embrace the multifaceted nature of interesting work in the real world.

There is not yet a definitive book for Cynefin but there are plenty of useful resources out there (for one thing, Dave is a prolific blogger). In *Kanban from the Inside* I touched on Cynefin in chapter 11, *Systems Thinking, Complexity, and the Learning Organisation*. Since then my friend Greg Brougham has produced this:

- *The Cynefin Mini-Book*
  Greg Brougham (2015, InfoQ)
  www.infoq.com/minibooks/cynefin-mini-book

See also:

- *A leader's framework for decision making*
  David J. Snowdon & Mary E. Boone
  (2007, Harvard Business Review)
  hbr.org/2007/11/a-leaders-framework-for-decision-making
- *Cynefin Review Part 7 – Finding Your Place on the Framework*
  Simon Powers (2016, Adventures with Agile blog)
  www.adventureswithagile.com/2016/04/11/cynefin-review-part-7-finding-your-place-on-the-framework/

A note on pronunciation: "Cynefin" is a Welsh word (it translates to "habitat" in English). It rhymes with "Kevin", and has the same initial hard consonant. As Liz Keogh (another friend) would say:

"Say *Kevin*. Now say *Cynefin*. Ku-NEV-in."

Plan on a page

An excellent resource for single-page and poster-sized representations of your highest-level plans for organisational change is Jason Little's book:

- *Lean Change Management: Innovative Practices For Managing Organizational Change*
  Jason Little (2014, Happy Melly Express)

Jason references another book in turn and I was grateful indeed for the pointer:

- *Mastering the Rockefeller Habits: What You Must Do to Increase the Value of Your Growing Firm*
  Verne Harnish (2002, Gazelles, Inc)

Despite the kind of title that might easily have put me off, I found something strangely familiar about this excellent book. My friend Karl Scotland helped me put my finger on it: Harnish's book was a strong influence on the founders of Rally Inc, Karl's former employer. I followed Rally's progress over the years via their company blog, and from time to time they gave us some very interesting insights into their strategic planning process. Karl himself is an expert in *Strategy Deployment*, a set of Lean techniques for creating strategic plans and aligning organisations around them.

Key points – 2. Exploration

Outputs:

- Completed assessment, online survey results
- Prioritised prompts and their respective obstacles
- More outcomes:
    - Generated from obstacles to prioritised assessment prompts using the 15-minute FOTO game introduced in Chapter 1

  o Organised (temporarily) using the Cynefin Four Points Contextualisation exercise

- A revision to the plan-on-a-page from Chapter 1

Concepts and tools:

- The Agendashift delivery assessment:

  o Descriptive instead of prescriptive

  o Organised by the values Transparency, Collaboration, Balance, Customer Focus, Flow, and Leadership

- The survey debrief – A well-tested walkthrough of survey results that helps to build a shared sense of how things are:

  o Overall and per-category score distributions and the key statistics of mode and median

  o Stronger and weaker categories, with perhaps a few of the strongest and weakest prompts

  o Areas of apparent agreement – consistency within categories and agreement on scores at prompt level

  o Areas of apparent disagreement – wide ranges of scores within categories and at prompt level, topics for more in-depth conversations

- Agreement first on priorities and then on outcomes

  o Outcomes generated via obstacles and the Clean Language game *15-minute FOTO* introduced in chapter 1

- The Cynefin Four Points Contextualisation exercise:

  o A great way to explore the very real need for different approaches to change

  o Reveals the four main Cynefin domains – Obvious, Complicated, Complex, and Chaos – together with a fifth domain, Disorder

- Related disciplines:
    - o 'Plan on a page'
    - o Lean Change Management
    - o Strategy Deployment

Chapter 3. Mapping

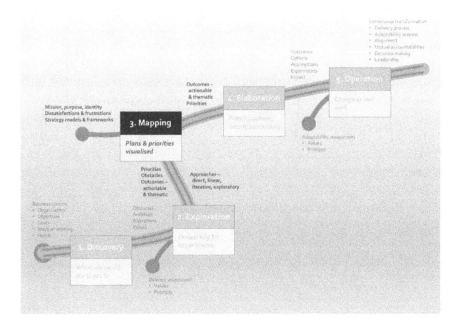

After Exploration, you have most of what you need in order to produce your *Transformation Map*, a high-level plan or agenda for change that organises visually the outcomes you hope to accomplish.

My early transformation maps consisted simply of columns of sticky notes – each sticky representing an outcome – under the six headings of Transparency, Balance, Collaboration, Customer Focus, Flow, and Leadership. Within each column, stickies were prioritised top to bottom.

It seemed an obvious enough approach, but I learned the hard way that plans built this way tend to be uncompelling, or worse. With headings like those, where are you supposed to start? Does Transparency necessarily come before Balance, and must both come before (say) Customer Focus and Leadership? Of course not. Instead of being inspired by the values, people were left confused.

The spine of our plan: A transformation journey

Revisiting the Agile technique of User Story Mapping (more on this later in the chapter) I was simultaneously reassured and concerned. Reassured, because I knew that my problem wasn't the simple visual structure of columns with headings. Concerned, because I understood that my problem was the complete lack of any sense of narrative flow across my headings, and where was that going to come from?

Ironically, I had overlooked a ready-made structure I have used to good effect since mid-2014 (I gave an early version of this brief coverage in my first book):

1. Refine existing work management systems

2. Improve the service experience

3. Manage the knowledge discovery process

4. Balance demand and capability

5. Address sources of dissatisfaction and other motivations for change

6. Pursue fitness for purpose

In terms of that essential narrative flow, you could say that this starts with the basics, ramps up the sophistication, and finishes with a flourish on bigger-picture organisational challenges and behaviours. With no more introduction than that, I usually let these headings and their respective prompts (the same prompts as the previous chapter but reorganised) speak for themselves. Here though, I will however share something of their intent as we work our way through them, and I will explain their origins later in the chapter.

1. Refine existing work management systems

Under this first heading we organise outcomes that relate to our day-to-day work management systems. We're looking to improve the surface detail – the tools, meetings, artefacts, and so on – that we use to coordinate our efforts and to keep our attention focused on the right things.

Four of the mini assessment's prompts (Chapter 2) fall quite naturally under this heading. They're drawn mainly from the Transparency category, with one from the Balance category also:

1.   (1.1) Our delivery process and the work items currently in progress within it are easily visible to all involved and interested parties

2.   (1.2) We have visibility of work items due to enter the delivery process soon

3.   (2.2) We maintain a clear separation between work currently in progress and work still under consideration

4.   (1.3) We can see which work items are blocked and for what reason

The numbers in parentheses – 1.1, 1.2, 2.2, and 1.3 – exist to ease the transition from the values-based structure we saw in the previous chapter. These prompt IDs let us switch easily between the two structures – surveying, debriefing, and so on in one and mapping in the other.

If you're familiar with a wide enough range of Lean-Agile techniques, methods, and process frameworks, you'll soon realise that these prompts are open to a wide variety of implementations. But before you jump too quickly to your favourite solutions, give everyone the chance to think about the outcomes they want to achieve.

Depending on how much work you have done already, there are two main approaches to map-building you can take here:

1.   Reuse the outputs of Exploration: gather together existing outcomes that now belong under this new heading

2. Work from scratch: put this category's prompts into priority order, identify their respective obstacles, and generate outcomes

Approach 1 (reuse) is the efficient choice if you've just completed Exploration, especially if you had the foresight to note prompt IDs (1.1, 1.2, etc) against each outcome. Approach 2 (generation) makes sense if you're refreshing an existing map or if you've decided that you'd like to start over.

Approach 2 is likely to generate a greater number of outcomes than option 1, and more is not necessarily better. Be prepared to prioritise ruthlessly! But regardless of approach, remain open to additional outcomes that are suggested by the category in general but don't seem to belong to any specific prompt.

Headings 2, 3, and 4 work in just the same way, and here's a facilitation tip: If you need to speed up the process you can work on all three (or more) headings together. We'll take headings 5 and 6 separately.

2. Improve the service experience

Under this second heading we organise outcomes related to our responsiveness to customers and our management of customer expectations. It's not technically difficult to score well against these two prompts, but it's surprising how few teams actually demonstrate these capabilities convincingly:

1. (5.1) We can predict with reasonable confidence how long it will take to deliver work of typical value and risk

2. (5.2) We understand the performance of our delivery system in sufficient detail to make timely decisions, to set appropriate expectations, and to focus our improvement efforts

These prompts – both from the Flow category – represent the basics. Adding some more challenge:

- Are you able to manage work of different types or different urgencies and offer predictable service for each?

- Does the timing of your deliveries owe more to internal convenience or to some misguided sense of efficiency than it does to customer value?

Anyway... You know the drill: Prompts, obstacles, outcomes, then more outcomes. If you're a fan of dodgy mnemonics you could remember this as POOO; I prefer the safer but still quite dodgy POWT:

- **Prompts** (or more generally, prioritised goals)

- **Obstacles** – things that stand in the way of those prompts being realised as you would like

- **What would you like to have happen?** Identify outcomes hiding behind those obstacles

- **Then what happens?** More outcomes, the outcomes behind the outcomes

3. Manage the knowledge discovery process

The premise of this third category is that the different stages of your delivery workflow each represent opportunities for different kinds of learning. With this in mind, you can optimise your process so that your most critical assumptions are tested soonest, you detect misunderstandings or quality problems at the earliest opportunity, and you get timely feedback from your customers and from other sources.

The relevant prompts from the mini assessment are shown below. As you might expect, the two original categories represented here are Collaboration and Customer Focus:

1. (3.1) We work with those whose needs we are meeting in order to understand, shape and size potential work before committing to deliver it

2. (4.1) We seek to align our work to shared goals, prioritising for maximum impact

3.   (4.2) We incorporate customer feedback into our work while it is in the delivery process

4.   (4.3) We continue to own work items until the customer confirms that their needs are being met

Nowhere in these four prompts (nor in any of the others, even in the full 43-prompt assessment) is there any suggestion that we should expect perfect inputs. This is deliberate. It's no coincidence either that we've also brought under one heading two prompts that relate to needs. A robust process is one that can receive incomplete, incorrect, contradictory, and downright misleading inputs and still manage to produce something that meets needs. Only a collaborative process can achieve this, and it's important that you challenge improvement ideas that amount to everyone else (customers included) doing their job more accurately.

4. Balance demand and capability

This category's two mini assessment prompts relate to how demand is balanced with the capacity and capability of the delivery system:

1.   (2.3) We take steps to avoid being overburdened with more work-in-progress than we can accommodate effectively

2.   (2.1) We bring work into the delivery process only as capacity allows, preferring to finish work items already in progress than to start new work items

These prompts align well with both the Agile outcome of *sustainable pace* and the Lean concept of *pull systems*. Balancing demand with capability is a broader concept however. You can include under this heading outcomes that relate to:

- Your overall mix of work – by type, stakeholder, time horizon, etc

- Your attitudes to demand – whether or not you assume that every request will be fulfilled, for example

- Your ability to improve the quality of your demand – by engaging proactively with its sources, taking steps to reduce unwanted demand, and so on

5. Address sources of dissatisfaction and other motivations for change

Under this heading we gather outcomes that represent the resolution of customer dissatisfaction and team frustration. Here we have from the mini assessment two Flow-related prompts that correspond with common sources of frustration (not just the emotion, but the sense that our efforts are frustrated by system shortcomings):

1.	(5.3) We proactively identify and address dependencies and other impediments to flow

2.	(3.2) Our delivery process encourages collaboration across roles and specialties

In this category these two prompts are just a starting point; more broadly this category is all about two kinds of current obstacles and their corresponding outcomes. If you wish, you can draw up two lists:

1.	Sources of customer dissatisfaction

2.	Sources of internal frustration

Spend a few minutes on each, writing down the sources of dissatisfaction and frustration you identify. Afterwards, treat them as obstacles and from those generate some positive outcomes.

Sometimes I facilitate this as a workshop exercise in its own right, and as I do so I like to display this picture (*Figure 22*) by my friend Markus Andrezak. As he puts it: at the same time as you raise self-awareness of what's happening inside your system, can you engender empathy with those who sit outside?

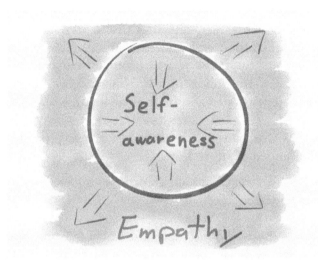

Figure 22 Empathy and self-awareness (source: Markus Andrezak, used with permission)

6. Pursue fitness for purpose

Let's begin this sixth and final category with another exercise. Like the dissatisfactions and frustrations exercise of the previous section it's a team exercise one you can do at any time:

- *1-4-All*-style – individually, then in pairs, then in table groups – describe *what you deliver, to whom, and why it matters*

- Now reflect:

  o How similar were the answers you shared? Where they differed, how coherent were they?

  o Could you have predicted the answers your colleagues produced?

- o Do you think you could predict the answers that your seniors, customers, and other stakeholders might give on your behalf?

- o Conversely, what would they make of any attempts by you to answer this on their behalf?

Optionally, you might discuss how you would measure success. Be aware though that the topic of metrics can easily provoke resistance and it is not always a good place to start, even if it is an important topic to be addressed when the time is right. Whatever you decide, don't risk losing sight of the fact that purpose is about more than numbers!

If this exercise raises any issues (eg of awareness, understanding, or alignment), capture them as obstacles and generate their respective outcomes in the usual way.

More generally, this category is a good place for outcomes that relate to clarity of purpose, organisational values, alignment (the degree to which you are all pulling in the same direction, contributing to the same ends), and longevity (long-term success, even across generations). Here are the relevant prompts from the mini assessment, the last four of the 18:

1. (3.3) We meet on a regular basis to review and improve our outputs and processes

2. (6.1) Together, we strive to meet customer needs, improve our delivery systems, and develop new capabilities; in all three pursuits we are appropriately recognised, supported, and rewarded

3. (6.3) We all share the responsibility to seek clarification, to highlight problems, and to come up with improvement ideas

4. (6.2) We ensure that opportunities for improvement are recognised and systematically followed through

Visualising your transformation map

Here (Figure 23) is an empty transformation map ready for population. In my preparations beforehand I wrote the category names on six large stickies for the headings (my handwriting wins no prizes); later I spread them out horizontally in a row near the top of our chosen space. Notice the room I left above them, a parking area for any stickies we weren't sure about.

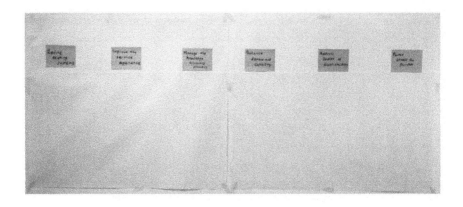

Figure 23 An empty transformation map

Participants worked in their small groups to generate their outcomes. Each time we had a category's worth of outcomes, we all gathered at the wall to review them as they are placed under their heading. As we placed them, we ranked them so that the outcomes of greatest and most urgent opportunity floated to the top of their respective columns. Of course, this isn't just about priority and sequence – it's how we make sure that everyone had the same understanding of what each outcome is about, what's involved, relative benefits, and relative urgency. These are important conversations!

76

The finished map looked like this (Figure 24):

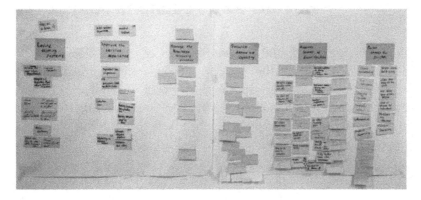

Figure 24 A completed transformation map

This map has some interesting features to point out. First, notice that some groups found it helpful to record on their stickies the ID number of the prompt that suggested the outcome (this is most apparent in the second column, *Improve the service experience*).

Second, notice the smaller stickies at the bottom of the fourth category, *Balance demand and capacity*. Here, the team felt it worth making visible the obstacles they wished to overcome.

Third, notice what to me is the most interesting feature here, the set of four stickies placed above the headings. They read:

- "Feel as a team" (smiley face)
- "Meet customer expectations"
- "Mindset culture"
- "Happy client"

These are examples of 'thematic outcomes', outcomes that might serve as better column headings. Opinions may vary on whether these will be fully achieved within any specific timescale. What's important here is coherence: actions that clearly support the theme and that add up to something meaningful, commensurate with the group's overall ambition.

Review and reconcile

By all means, step back and admire the fruit of your collective labours once you've completed the process of generating, organising, and prioritising outcomes. But do then review it carefully. As with all reviews, the hardest part is to spot what's missing, and an effective way to do this is to reconcile it with other artefacts or models. I will suggest two reconciliations here and introduce a third at the end of the chapter.

For the first reconciliation, check your transformation map against your plan-on-a-page from the preceding chapter. How does your more detailed plan stack up against the ambitions you previously articulated? Does it take you the whole way? It might be ok if it doesn't – perhaps the new plan has a shorter time horizon than the first one – but are you omitting anything essential?

The second reconciliation could be dubbed "one model to the tune of another". Take your plan, and use a completely different model as a cross-check. One of many possible models is my own, my *6 leadership strategies* model (see Resources):

1. **Skills-first**: Does your plan include developing, hiring, or otherwise obtaining all the skills needed to realise your ambition?

2. **Process-first**: Will your plan bring into being the kind of process that you want? An anticipatory, *right-people-right-conversations-best-possible-moment* kind of process, both within teams and across teams (assuming that all of this is in scope here)?

3. **Needs-first**: Will you be putting those skills and process together deliberately to explore, prioritise, anticipate, and meet needs, and to validate that you are doing this successfully? Are you prepared no longer to accept requirements at face value?

4. **Improvement-driven**: Do you have the people, the management commitment, the mutual accountabilities, the regular feedback, and the safety necessary to sustain the improvement/transformation process you are starting here?

5. **Alignment-driven**: What mechanisms will keep everyone pulling in the same direction? If they don't exist already, what plans do you have for putting them in place?

6. **Purpose-driven**: Is there sufficient shared understanding of why the organisation exists and what it needs to become? What role does your plan play in realising that?

If you don't have all the right people in the room you may find questions like these difficult to answer. That's not a reason to give up! Log your outstanding questions, and as you wrap up, make sure that each question has an owner and an agreed timeframe for reporting back. You may find that some of your questions will be answered as you begin Elaboration and Operation (the next two chapters).

Before we leave these strategies I will mention that some of them will be echoed in some deeper leadership principles which we'll explore in chapter 5. For example, underpinning *skills-first* is a kind of social contract of *mutual accountability*: I (as your manager or coach) won't expect you do something you've not done before without also taking some appropriate level of responsibility for your capability to do it. To put it more strongly, my neglect should not cause you to be set up for failure.

Choose what's next

You can't do everything all at once, and the last Mapping task (at least for now) is to choose a small number of outcomes to carry forward into Elaboration. Each group should make its own choices, keeping in mind:

1. You should already have a rough priority order within each category, highest priority outcomes at the top

2. Broadly, your categories are sequenced from left to right in order of the degree of organisational challenge involved

In general, you should aim to choose from your highest priority items. If you're not sure how to get started, expect to find some of your most actionable outcomes in the leftmost categories. Watch out though for dependencies – don't start what you can't finish! Do your top priority outcomes have some natural ordering? Do they need to be preceded by 'enabling' outcomes that you haven't yet prioritised?

Notice that your map's narrative flow doesn't dictate priorities. You aren't going to complete all of column 1 before moving onto column 2, for example. It's a bit like editing a movie: you can push inconsequential details to the background (better still, remove them completely), and you have the power to choose the order in which the key moments are tackled. Some of the best movies start with a foretaste of the ending, so why can't you?

Here (Figure 25), selected items have been flagged with small stickies in a contrasting colour. Notice how they form a 'slice' across the map; this is a very common pattern. They'll be the first to go through Elaboration (next chapter).

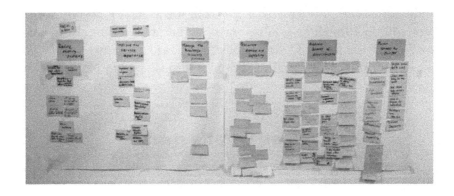

Figure 25 Outcomes selected for Elaboration

Behind the scenes

Reverse STATIK and the *Pathway edition* assessment template

The transformation map's initial headings come from a model called Reverse STATIK. In essence it's the *Systems Thinking Approach to Implementing Kanban* (STATIK – David J. Anderson's model and my mnemonic) but presented backwards. It's as though we are retracing our steps and looking for improvement opportunities that we might previously have missed.

1. Refine existing work management systems

2. Improve the service experience

3. Manage the knowledge discovery process

4. Balance demand and capability

5. Address sources of dissatisfaction and other motivations for change

6. Pursue fitness for purpose

In the original, "forward" version of STATIK, the final step is to design a context-specific kanban system, a visual management system that controls work in progress (WIP) in order to improve flow. In the reverse model, we begin with improvements to systems currently in place (in whatever form they happen to take), more clearly representing the start of an iterative, *start with what you do now* approach.

The *pathway edition* assessment template of this chapter (to give it the name we use to distinguish it from the 'original edition' of the previous chapter) is just the template of the previous chapter reorganised under these new headings. In the full-length version, one 'original' prompt is split between two categories in its corresponding pathway edition; no other edits were required.

User story mapping

A huge inspiration for the transformation map is the *user story map* (often just *story map*) as described in this excellent book that is also a great introduction to Agile:

- *User Story Mapping: Discover the Whole Story, Build the Right Product* Jeff Patton and Peter Economy (2014, O'Reilly Media)

In a user story map, the *spine* of the map (the headings) summarises one or more high level user journeys. The spine provides the map both with structure and with a sense of left-to-right flow. The "ribs" below the spine contain the detail of the journey steps, in the form of *user stories*.

User stories aren't complete specifications. In the words of Kent Beck, their inventor, user stories are just "placeholders for a conversation". Often those conversations start in a deliberately stereotyped way, conforming to a user story template such as this one, known as the Connextra template in honour of its source:

- As a *<persona>*, I want *<goal/desire>* so that *<benefit>*

In the transformation map, we're organising outcomes, ie just the *<benefit>* part of the story. A placeholder for a placeholder, if you like!

The needs behind the stories

In product development, user stories typically represent some aspect of a desired product feature that we wish to build or refine, as viewed from a single persona's perspective, and in the context of some specific benefit that they'd like to achieve. This narrowing of focus is immensely helpful in identifying small and independently testable units of work.

If we're not careful though, we might start to think like this:

- As the product team, we want *<feature>* so that *<business justification>*

I call this 'requirements thinking', and it's the start of a dangerous slippery slope towards mediocre products that satisfy no-one. To steer the conversation towards the 'needs thinking' that underpins several of the assessment prompts, you might try the *job story* template:

- When *<authentic situation of need>*, I want to *<action>* so I can *<achieve outcome>*

Of course the template isn't the real issue. For every user story (or equivalent) that you work with, are you able to describe an *authentic situation of need?* When and where does this feature matter to the persona identified in the story? Whose needs are we really prioritising? If the answers to these questions aren't immediately apparent – or worse, the answers are embarrassing – it's possible that you have a serious problem. Tick off as many requirements as you like, but if you're not meeting needs, what's the point?

Other maps: Impact maps and the X-matrix

Just a brief mention of two other mapping tools you may wish to consider, *impact maps* and the *X-matrix*.

Impact maps are described in this book:

- *Impact Mapping: Making a big impact with software products and projects*
  Gojko Adzic (2012, Provoking Thoughts)

Through their loose hierarchy of *goals, actors, impact,* and *behaviours* or *deliverables* (the latter shown Figure *26*), you can use impact mapping to explore questions such as these:

- Who shares these goals?

- In what measureable ways might these actors change their behaviour if their needs were better met?

- In support of the goals and the behaviour changes we hope to see, what should we do?

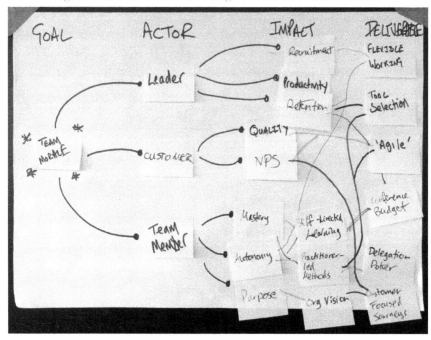

Figure 26 Example impact map

The X-matrix is a Lean tool for Strategy Deployment. Instead of the impact map's hierarchical organisation, the X-matrix (Figure 27) facilitates a four-way reconciliation exercise. The four dimensions to be reconciled are application-dependent, but something like this would be appropriate in a transformation context:

1. Aspirations versus strategies

2. Strategies versus tactics

3. Tactics versus evidence

4. Evidence versus aspirations

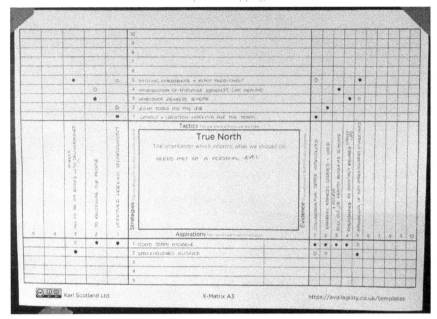

Figure 27 Example X-Matrix

Prefix those particular reconciliations with *True North* (there's space in the middle of the X-matrix where one can be written down) and you spell TASTE. Karl Scotland (who created the model) describes it in this blog post:

- *TASTE Success with an X-Matrix Template*
  (availagility.co.uk/2017/01/06/taste-success-with-an-x-matrix-template/)

You can download from there a template similar to the one shown in the photo.

X-matrices can get rather unwieldy when they contain a large number of items, but you may find it helpful to create a summary version using selected outputs from Discovery and Exploration as your aspirations, and relevant outcomes from Mapping as your strategies. Seeing where the gaps lie (strategies without tactics, aspirations without evidence) may help you prioritise outcomes for Elaboration (next chapter).

Is it Good Strategy?

To finish this chapter, the promised third reconciliation. This time, a quick check against Rumelt's *strategy kernel*. This model comes from another brilliant book:

- *Good Strategy/Bad Strategy:*
  The difference and why it matters
  Richard Rumelt (2011, Profile Books)

Three questions (Rumelt's model in bold, my commentary):

1. **Diagnosis**: Is your strategy rooted in an understanding of the challenge you face and the opportunities available?

2. **Guiding policy**: What gives shape to your strategy?

3. **Coherent actions**: Are your planned actions coherent with each other, your guiding policy, and your diagnosis?

By virtue of your transformation map's construction you should be able to give positive answers to questions 1 and 2, and a partial answer to question 3:

1. **Diagnosis?** Witness the obstacles and their respective outcomes from Discovery, Exploration, and Mapping (chapters 1-3) together with the survey analysis that informed Exploration (chapter 2).

2. **Guiding policy?** Your strategy was given shape first by the values and prompts of the assessment (chapter 2), and then by the transformation journey steps of this chapter.

3. **Coherent actions?** You have identified detailed outcomes and reconciled them with broader goals. Moreover, most (if not all) those outcomes align with one or more of the values of the assessment, and those values are themselves coherent.

Furthermore, you could add to point 3 that your overall approach to the transformation process is highly coherent with Lean-Agile sensibilities. Hardly a minor point!

So we're good then? Not so fast. A solid basis for a good strategy certainly, but a further level of detail is still required. We've said what we want to have happen, not the concrete steps we will take and what impact we think they will make. Cue chapter 4, Elaboration.

Key points – 3. Mapping

Outputs:

- Your agenda for change visualised as a *Transformation Map*:

  o Uses the format of the *User Story Map* with a default 'spine' or 'narrative flow' borrowed from *Reverse STATIK*

  o The spine provides the headings to columns of stickies and has a left to right flow

  o The stickies represent outcomes that align to their respective headings, and are prioritised top to bottom

Concepts and tools:

- Alternative mapping tools include *Impact Mapping* and *X-matrix*

- Take time to explore:

  o Sources of customer dissatisfaction and team frustration

  o *What you deliver, to whom, and why it matters –* and how these align between different people and teams

- Advice applicable both to product development and transformation:

  o Visualise your priorities, identifying your 'key moments'; implementation doesn't have to be linear

  o Replace mediocre 'requirements thinking' with 'needs thinking' by identifying *authentic situations of need*

- Reconcile your map with other sources:

- o Your own, such as your outputs from Discovery

- o Existing strategy models, for example *6 leadership strategies* and Rumelt's *strategy kernel*

Chapter 4. Elaboration

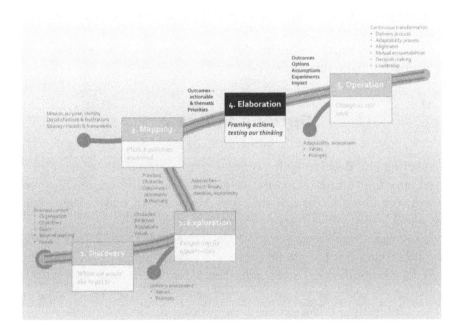

Cast your mind back to 2015. Even if you weren't a user at that time, it was hard to avoid the news reports suggesting that Facebook was about to augment its iconic 'Like' button, perhaps – shock! – with a 'Dislike' button.

You can imagine a product manager pitching the initial idea:

> "We believe that adding a Dislike button will result in increased engagement. If successful, we would expect to see more likes and dislikes recorded, more posts, more comments, and users spending more time in Facebook. All of these together will drive greater advertising revenue."

If ever such a pitch did take place, I wasn't there to witness it. Neither did I witness the process that led ultimately to the launch in early 2016 of Facebook's new 'Reactions' feature. We do however know that this hypothesis-driven style pioneered by startup companies is now very well established, spreading even to the government services sector (I saw this first-hand as interim delivery manager for two UK Government digital services).

Interestingly, much of the formalism that underpins this style comes originally not from the product development space, but from the process improvement space. The product development folks have however done much to make this knowledge easily accessible, and we're going to take full advantage.

Options thinking

Generating and developing hypotheses takes a little bit of effort. Not a huge amount relative to the effort of actually conducting an experiment, but still enough that it makes sense to make ensure that this initial effort will be focused somewhere worthwhile.

If you're trying this for the first time, a good definition of 'worthwhile' involves a combination of two ingredients:

1. Interesting – illustrative of the process and its possibilities

2. Valuable – likely to deliver practical benefit

The next two exercises are designed to maximise both interest and value by choosing the right kind of outcome and generating a range of options.

Create some options

The final task of Mapping (Chapter 3) was to choose some outcomes – valuable, presumably – to take forward into Elaboration. For the sake of illustration, we're going to work on just one. To make this interesting, we want one that might be approached from several directions. If that doesn't describe any of your prioritised outcomes, go back to your transformation map and choose another from there. You may already have identified and marked some suitable stickies at the end of the *Four Points* exercise of Chapter 2 – likely candidates would have been placed in or near to the *complex* (top left) domain.

Now generate some action ideas that will take you towards your chosen outcome. Make these as varied as you can – not just alternative solutions, but radically different *kinds* of solution. For example, if you come up with a tool-centric idea, try to think of a different approach – not just an alternative technology, but one that isn't tool-centric at all. If you come up with an idea that implies that the problem is someone else's responsibility, generate another where it's yours instead.

For example:

- Counter "Implement a communications system" with "Get out more"

- Counter "Reject bad requirements" with "Engage sooner upstream"

Real diversity comes from engaging multiple people in this process. The 1-2-4-All pattern (Chapter 2) is a great way to facilitate this:

- Each table group chooses an outcome to work with

- Working silently, each participant generates a range of ideas on their own

- Those ideas are compared, prioritised, combined, and refined – first in pairs, then in table groups

- Finally, each table group shares their shortlist of 3-5 ideas for wider discussion

By design, there's not much room here for prescription, or for the kind of so-called expert that will tell you that there's only one way to do it, often without trying to understand your context. But that's no reason to struggle on alone if you're running out of ideas! If you're not happy with your range of options, seek out answers to these questions:

1. What has worked elsewhere?

2. What would experts from different backgrounds recommend?

If you need external help, look for advisers who are able to give you multiple options, speak positively about several of them, and suggest which ones are most likely to be effective in different situations.

Consider your options

Which of these ideas should be taken forward? A good question and one that can be difficult to answer, in part because there are so many ways in which you could try to answer it. A great way to start to answer it is with another question:

"What would have to be true for this option to look fantastic?"

For the record, the originator of that question is Roger L. Martin, until 2013 the Dean of the Rotman School of Management at the University of Toronto. I found it in *Playing to Win, how Strategy Really Works* (Boston: Harvard Business Press), which Martin co-authored with A. G. Lafley, former head of Proctor & Gamble.

First of all, consider the 'best case scenario' for each of your action ideas (your options). Are they capable of being 'fantastic', delivering benefits that very significantly outweigh the costs involved? Discard any incapable options. Consider also the best case scenario for 'option zero', the option of doing nothing. If this no-action option has some fantastic potential, add it to your list.

Next, for each of your remaining action ideas, make a list of all the things that would need to be true for that option to deliver that hoped-for degree of upside. This list may include:

- Things under your control

- Things that you will come to depend on later

- Things "out there" that you're not sure of at this time but could perhaps find out

- Things that will always be hard to predict

- Things that may remain essentially unknowable until the last (or worst) moment

How fantastic do your options look after you have accounted for their likelihood of success? You might characterise them as solid and boring (not likely to be fantastic, but still reliable), exciting but risky (high potential, but perhaps more likely to fail than to succeed), or not worth the trouble (little to no chance of success). If you generate enough ideas against enough outcomes, you'll soon have a good mixture – a healthy *options portfolio*, if you like – even after eliminating the duds.

For the purposes of this exercise, the interesting options are the ones that have some genuine uncertainties to explore. Ignoring any boring options, select one to take further.

Hypothesis-driven change

To *elaborate* your action ideas, in other words to develop them in sufficient detail that you can be reasonably confident that they can and (importantly) should be implemented, we will use a combination of new and traditional techniques. The new comes from Lean Startup, the body of knowledge developed and employed by the startup community, as invoked in my Facebook example at the opening of this chapter. The old is a mixture of A3 – a technique developed at Toyota and adopted by the Lean community – and a light sprinkling of good old-fashioned project management (think PMI, PMBOK, etc).

But before we start, we must pay careful heed to a core principle of Lean, the concept of *just-in-time* (JIT) production. Do not try to elaborate all of your action ideas up front. Any attempt to do so would be:

1. wasteful – some of the ideas you'll be documenting won't be implemented any time soon (if ever), and

2. madness – you couldn't possibly predict the conditions under which they will all (eventually) be implemented, especially when you are in the business of making change happen!

If you're doing elaboration just-in-time, it means that you're doing just enough work at just the right time to enable you to make effective decisions when they need to be made – no more and no less, no sooner and no later. You're doing enough to avoid starving later activities of high quality work, but not so much that you delay important decisions or risk losing relevance entirely.

Framing your hypothesis

Recall the Facebook example from the top of the chapter:

> "We believe that adding a Dislike button will result in increased engagement. If successful, we would expect to see more likes and dislikes recorded, more posts, more comments, and users spending more time in Facebook. All of these together will drive greater advertising revenue."

I created that hypothesis from this template (lightly editing it to make it sound like something someone might actually have said out loud):

- We believe that *<actionable change>* will result in *<meaningful outcome>*. *for Sheet*

    If successful, we might expect to see:

    o   *<observable impact>*

    o   ...

    o   *<observable impact>*

There are a number of different variants of this template in circulation. Some emphasise strict quantitative tests that will determine success or failure unequivocally. Others (like this one) are more relaxed – more accepting of qualitative observation, and more open to human judgement on whether (in retrospect) the change should be adopted as an improvement.

I tend towards the 'relaxed' school here for a number of reasons: partly to make the template more broadly applicable and appealing, partly to emphasise the humility that goes with expressing our actions as hypotheses, and partly because it stops unnecessarily high hurdles being placed in the way of change. Better to risk an occasional lapse in rigour than to stop change in its tracks.

Try it: Take one of your more promising action ideas and the outcome it was generated for, and complete the first sentence of the hypothesis template, adjusting your wording as necessary:

- We believe that *<actionable change>*
  will result in *<meaningful outcome>*.

Be honest now: Is *<meaningful outcome>* a realistic description of what you can hope to achieve from your *<actionable change>*? If it isn't, adjust accordingly and remember that further work will be required after this one.

Now for the second part of the template:

- If successful, we might expect to see:

  o   *<observable impact>*

  o   ...

  o   *<observable impact>*

Don't settle for just one *<observable impact>*; aim for several. You might find these (non-core) Clean Language questions helpful:

- *What's happening when [change in X]?* (Eg: What's happening when increased engagement?)

- *What's the first thing that lets you know [change in X]?* (Eg: What's the first thing that lets you know increased engagement?)

Generally, it's advisable to focus first on changes in behaviour, and then on ways you might observe and measure them. In the Facebook example, the behaviour changes are people registering their likes and dislikes, entering posts and comments, spending time in Facebook, etc. The rates of clicks, comments, etc are easily measurable. *"Greater advertising revenue"* is also measurable, but it might be hard to prove that this improvement is directly attributable to this change (which isn't to say that it isn't worth trying).

Developing your hypothesis: the A3 template

Your hypothesis belongs in one section (upper left) of our A3 template (Figure *28*). The A3 doesn't need much introduction at this stage other than to say:

- It's named after the paper size (and I really do keep a supply of these printed on A3 paper)

- If Toyota thinks that one sheet of A3 is enough paper to scope a change (however big that change may be), then it's good enough for me

- This particular template (available under a Creative Commons license – see Resources) will serve our immediate needs well but there are many others to choose from (it is said that there are as many A3 templates as there are Lean consultants)

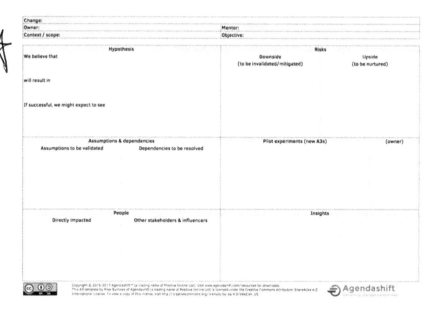

Figure 28 The Agendashift A3 template

We'll now go through the A3 section by section.

Assumptions and dependencies

Assumptions & dependencies	
Assumptions to be validated	Dependencies to be resolved

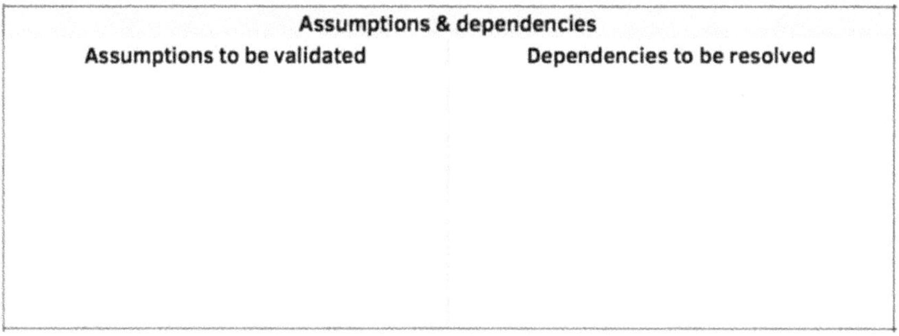

Figure 29 Assumptions and dependencies

Take the list you prepared of everything that will need to be true for your action idea to *be fantastic*. For your A3, divide your list into two:

1. **Assumptions** – things that you don't yet know; things that are not yet *proven or validated* (and might yet be disproved or invalidated instead)

2. **Dependencies** – things that aren't yet in place for a demonstrably successful implementation

"Proven or validated" comes from the standard PMBOK definition (PMBOK is an acronym for the Project Management Body of Knowledge).

The line between assumptions and dependencies can sometimes be a little blurry. If you need to help to decide, consider the effort implied by the *"not yet"*. If that effort will be focussed mainly on establishing the truth of something, it's an assumption. If the effort will be focussed mainly on putting something in place or on coordinating with other people, it's a dependency.

For example:

- Assumption: The customer will want to attend our proposed meetings at the frequency we desire

- Dependencies: Our meetings' exact timing and format, the agreed design of any required artefacts, and the participation of our colleagues

Pilot experiments

Pilot experiments (new A3s)	(owner)

Figure 30 Pilot experiments

Hypothesis-driven change isn't just about how we frame our big ideas, it's also about how we make progress. We can think of each assumption and dependency as representing an opportunity for experimentation. And the opportunity can be enormous, because these *pilot experiments* will generally be executed much more quickly and cheaply than the overall experiment, with potentially massive savings not only in time and money, but in reputation too.

Can you think of some quick and cheap ways to validate (or invalidate) each of your assumptions? Which assumption would you test first? What would constitute a successful test, and what would you do if it failed? Similarly, which of your dependencies represent the most serious impediments to progress? Can you think of ways to mitigate them quickly?

Examples:

- Agree a regular diary slot with the customer
- Circulate a proposed standing agenda for comment
- Establish a quorum of internal participants

Achieve even just the first of these and you're already making progress!

Discuss your pilot experiments, summarise them on the A3, and be prepared to break out new A3s for the most challenging of them.

Finally, are there any other steps you will need to remember – approvals, implementation steps, documentation changes, and the like? Make a note of them here. Don't be afraid to include the obvious and the complicated here – the former so that they're not forgotten and the latter as a placeholder for more detailed planning.

Do you have a baseline?

In my definition of dependencies, I should perhaps have highlighted the word *"demonstrably"*. If your idea turns out to be fantastically successful, it will be obvious enough to everyone. Even in these happy circumstances, wouldn't it be great if you could quantify its impact somehow?

What if it were only moderately successful? How then would you know? And how sure can you be at the start that it is actually worth doing? Can you imagine a dataset that would tell you even before you changed anything whether the opportunity is as big as you think it is?

A *baseline* is just a measurement (or set of measurements) against which you can later make comparisons. If you're struggling to identify assumptions, dependencies, and pilot experiments, they can be a great source of inspiration:

- If you don't have the data yet, plan an experiment to resolve this dependency

- If you don't know for sure what the data will look like, make some assumptions about it that you can test

- Assuming that you will have the data, design an experiment that would demonstrate an improvement unequivocally

Risks

Risks	
Downside (to be invalidated/mitigated)	**Upside** (to be nurtured)

Figure 31 Risks – upside and downside

This section of the A3 is about the uncertainty that accompanies change to complex systems. We seek to identify two types of uncertainty in particular:

- **Downside risks** – possible negative consequences

- **Upside risks** – possible benefits beyond those that we're pursuing explicitly, the 'potential for fantastic' if you like

It's important to identify downside risks for the obvious reason that we should have plans in place for dealing with them, even if that plan is to accept rather than mitigate the consequences. It's good to ask questions like these:

- What could go wrong?

- What possible unintended consequences could there be?

- Is this experiment *safe to fail?* Are we putting personal or corporate reputations, capital, careers, or health at unacceptable risk?

Not all risks are bad however. Often, the worst that happens is that we learn something, and the more prepared we are, the more we'll learn.

And there may be "risks to the upside", as my former colleagues in the investment banking world might say. Don't ignore the potential upsides; they're much more likely to flourish if the "green shoots" are recognised, nurtured, and encouraged to spread and multiply.

Reviewing your downside and upside risks, should you plan some additional pilot experiments? Can you think of ways in which you might obtain the learning and the upsides without incurring the downsides?

People

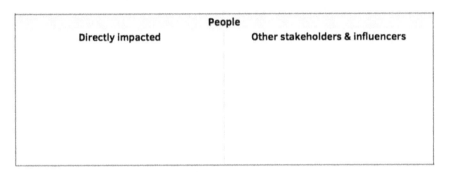

Figure 32 People

Hypotheses, assumptions, dependencies, pilot experiments, risks... all very technical! Let's not forget that change involves people:

- Impacted – people who will need to do things differently

- Implementers – people making the change happen on the ground

- Influencers – people whose support will help make the change happen

- Customers and others who stand to benefit

- Anyone who might hold a veto

- Managers and other senior staff involved in governance – they're people too!

In the easiest cases, these groups overlap significantly, with the people impacted also making it happen, surrounded by supporters, receiving some direct benefit, and able to make decisions for themselves. Even in these easy cases, and crucially when you don't have this natural advantage, go no further until you have identified who these people are. Can you enlist them as supporters? Could they have some fresh understanding to offer? Can they help you test your ideas on paper before anything more risky or expensive is tried?

Insights

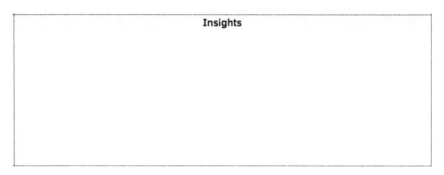

Figure 33 Insights

The last section in the main body of the A3 is labelled *Insights*. Leave this blank for now, but imagine for a moment the insights you might hope to capture here after your hypothesis has been tested. Are your pilot experiments capable of generating the insights you seek? Could you generate them more quickly, more cheaply, or more safely some other way?

The fact that you can't fill in this section right away has some important implications. How do you prevent your A3 from just gathering dust in a drawer? How do you ensure follow-through? I'll leave those questions hanging for now; we'll address these issues in the next chapter.

Alternative approaches

For the bulk of this chapter you were working with an outcome deliberately chosen to suit an experimental, hypothesis-driven approach. Is such an approach always appropriate?

The honest answer is no, but there are good reasons for making it the baseline approach against which more focussed approaches can be understood:

- It's safer than using plan-driven or ad-hoc approaches inappropriately
- It is easy to adapt

Suppose you had chosen to work with an outcome placed near the *obvious*, *complicated*, or *chaos* corners in the Cynefin Four Points contextualization exercise of Chapter 2? What should you have done differently? Let's take those one at a time.

Obvious

If you can document and track your changes with nothing more sophisticated than marker pens and sticky notes, do it! Just make sure first that it really is an obvious change. It's not enough that it seems obvious just to you; broad agreement should be easy to obtain, so there's no excuse for taking shortcuts here.

Were you to decide to complete an A3 for an obvious outcome, almost the worst thing that can happen is that you waste a few pointless minutes filling in a template, pointless because everything you write is already well known or of little consequence. Annoying perhaps, but no disaster.

I say "almost the worst" as a warning against bureaucracy. It would be unfortunate indeed if obvious but still worthwhile changes were continually stifled by demands for documentation. There is a countermeasure to this: agree local policies for recognising and dealing with obvious changes. This improvement might itself be a candidate for an A3!

Complicated

For changes that are only moderately complicated (borderline obvious), the Agendashift A3 template works fine: just use the pilot experiments section to document the key steps of the plan. For more complicated changes, delegate someone to find and complete a more appropriate template (there are plenty to choose from) or to start with a blank page. For the most complicated changes, use the A3 as tool for thinking and presentation, with the detail managed elsewhere.

Chaos

With or without A3, there are no easy solutions when you're in the chaos corner. Keep your experiments simple until your understanding and confidence grows. Record your observations and insights, even if at first it's hard to see direct relationships between the actions you take and what you later observe. If time is of the essence you may have to act first and reflect later; just don't neglect the reflection part.

Allow your thinking to be tested

One element that should be common to any A3 is the header section (Figure *34*).

Figure 34 The A3 template's header section

The key requirements here:

- Basic summary information that makes each A3 easily to identify and cross-reference

- Identification of the person or people responsible for maintaining and executing the A3

- Identification of the mentor (a coach, manager, or experienced colleague) whose job is to challenge and guide both the thinking captured in the A3 and the actions that follow from it

Given that in early drafts it's likely that important things will have been overlooked, the mentor's most powerful question is probably *"What else?"*. After that, it's *"Then what happens?"*, inviting comparison between this experiment's likely outcomes, the initial outcome against which this experiment was first proposed, and the 'fantastic' scenario that helped prioritise it. Typically there are gaps at outcome level too, and more ambitious outcomes have the potential to generate a significant number of experiments. Not that this should come as a surprise – Rome wasn't built in a day!

In complex cases it pays to allow your thinking to be tested in this way repeatedly. By definition, your outcome is not of a kind amenable to a linear process of analysis, planning, and execution. There is no straight line march towards your outcome; instead you iterate towards it, learning, building, watching the gaps as they shrink and grow, and delivering value as you go. Robust mentoring isn't to help you create the perfect plan, it is to keep you focussed both on your goals and your most important next steps.

Behind the scenes

Lean Startup

Some of the language may be new, but the application of hypotheses to process and organisational change was well established even by the late 1940's. Thanks to the quality movement, to Toyota, and to Lean, these practices could almost be described as mainstream now.

Lean Startup "reimagined" these well-established ideas so that they could gain an exciting new lease of life in environments of rapid product development and evolution, such as may be found in young (and nowadays not so young) internet companies and other startups. It was quickly recognised that these new-look tools continued to work well not just for product development teams but for their host organisations too, and they spread quickly to other communities, the Agile community included. There is a kind of "product/process duality" at work here, and it should not be surprising: the process *is* the product when customers buy into product potential as well as current product capability. Tools that work for one often work for the other.

It's a matter of personal taste and not a criticism that I choose to stick with the more modern toolset. For example, there's nothing fundamentally wrong with older tools such as the PDSA (or PDCA) cycle:

- **Plan** an experiment
- **Do** (conduct) it
- **Study** (or **Check**) the results
- Decide whether and how to **Act** (or to **Adopt** a change)
- Rinse and repeat

However, I find it helpful to treat these two main disciplines separately:

1. How to frame and develop experiments (as described in this chapter)
2. How to manage their execution (the next chapter).

Lean Startup doesn't insist on this separation, but it has certainly made it easier.

Recommended reading:

- *Running Lean: Iterate from plan A to a plan that works*
  Ash Maurya (2012, O'Reilly Media)
- *The Lean Startup: How constant innovation creates radically successful businesses*
  Eric Ries (2011, Portfolio Penguin)

A3

A3 is important not just as a prominent Toyota artefact embraced by the community but for what it reveals of Toyota's underlying management philosophy and its approach to leadership development. This makes it well worth studying, and I recommend these books:

- *Managing to Learn: Using the A3 management process to solve problems, gain agreement, mentor, and lead*
  John Shook (2010, Lean Enterprise Institute)

- *Understanding A3 Thinking: A Critical Component of Toyota's PDCA Management System*
  Durward K. Surbek II & Art Smalley
  (2008, Productivity Press)

Solutions Focus

Solutions Focus is a coaching discipline that's a good fit for Agendashift generally and for the options generation part most especially. The name may be slightly misleading: it is very much a *start with what you do now* approach, the 'solutions' being expressions of "what's wanted" or "ways forward" rather than designs to implement, the coach helping the client to identify what may be working already and resources that may already be available to them.

There are other resonances with Agendashift:

- Like Clean Language, a heritage in psychotherapy

- A strong bias away from digging deep into obstacles, working instead towards identifying positive possibilities (this being regarded as typically the more productive approach in complex environments)

- Discovery tools that help to 'appreciate the best of what is' (see also *Appreciative Enquiry*) and generate optimism for the future

- *Scaling*, here meaning the use of numerical scales such as 0-10 or 1-4 and other informal measures of progress; if you score something a 2 (say), you accept that it's not a 3, and sometimes that's important

Book recommendation:

- *The Solutions Focus: Making Coaching and Change SIMPLE*
  Mark McKergow and Paul Z. Jackson (2nd edition 2011,
  Nicholas Brealey International)

Toyota Kata

My last book recommendation for this chapter has spawned an
enthusiastic sub-community of its own:

- *Toyota Kata: Managing People for Improvement, Adaptiveness and
  Superior Results*
  Mike Rother (2009, McGraw-Hill)

20th century Lean suffered from a problem that 21st century Lean has
come to acknowledge and address: transplanting tools from one
organisational context to another is not something to be done lightly,
even when the source of those tools is Toyota, the company that was
Lean's inspiration. The Lean movement has learned the hard way that
copying the surface detail without paying attention to the supporting
infrastructure is a recipe for fragility, not sustainability.

Great care must be taken when you're taking tools from one domain
into another. For example, to make the transition from automotive
manufacturing into creative knowledge work, Kanban needed not just
tweaks but a radical reimagining. However, and even if you share my
real discomfort when the manufacturing production line is invoked as
a metaphor for other kinds of work, the best of the Lean literature is
well worth studying. *Toyota Kata* is a particularly rewarding read if (i)
you're comfortable with Lean terminology or are interested in learning
some, and (ii) you're ready to look beyond the tools to the principles
that underpin them.

Here too you'll notice a number of parallels with Agendashift:

- Goals, obstacles, outcomes – elicited and even named differently, but a similar kind of structure

- Analogous to our use of Clean Language, practised coaching routines, the *kata* of the title (think the *Karate Kid's* "Wax on, wax off" for a fictional example with the same Japanese roots)

- The use of hypotheses and experiments

- The vital role of supportive management systems and the thinking that underpins them

We'll put management systems under the spotlight in Chapter 5, Operation, the next and final chapter.

Key points – 4. Elaboration

Outputs:

- An A3 template completed for one option:
  - Hypothesis
  - Assumptions and dependencies
  - Pilot experiments
  - Risks – upside and downside
  - People
  - Insights (hoped for)

Concepts and tools:

- When appropriate, a hypothesis-driven approach to elaboration:
  - Start with a high priority outcome likely to be amenable to alternative approaches
  - Generate a diverse range of options
  - Frame your most promising option as a hypothesis (Lean Startup style)

- o Develop it in the form of an A3 (Lean style), generating lower level pilot experiments as required, covering assumptions and dependencies, risks (to the upside as well as the downside), and people

- o Consider baseline data

- o Review experiments up front for their ability to generate the insights you seek

- For some outcomes, other approaches may be more appropriate:

  - o A direct, low-overhead approach when the solution is obvious to all concerned

  - o Analysis and a more linear process of planning and execution may be delegated to qualified people if the selected outcome can safely be expected to be delivered that way

  - o As per chapter 2, these approaches aren't always mutually exclusive

- Related coaching frameworks:

  - o Solutions Focus, a coaching framework that like Clean Language has roots in psychotherapy

  - o Toyota Kata, a Lean coaching framework

Chapter 5. Operation

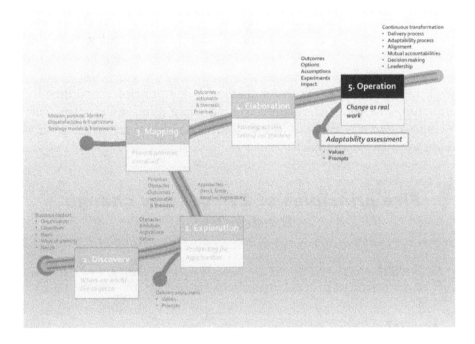

Well done! You have your transformation map and you've agreed your top priority outcomes. You know how to generate options, to frame hypotheses, and to develop your experiments to an appropriate level of detail. Plenty there to be getting on with!

"I can't wait to get started!" is the sentiment often expressed at this stage. That's great of course, and let's not waste that new-found energy. Yes, do get cracking, but do it with your eyes open, aware that you're approaching a fork in the road.

The easy path is represented by your priority list: you do the obvious thing and share out some actions. The all-too-familiar result is that just a few of the easiest changes get made, and soon you find yourself needing to reboot the process all over again – a disappointing return on all that effort! But there's a path of opportunity too: one that opens up when the focus is not only on agreed actions but also on how the follow-through will be managed towards self-perpetuation. Instead of enabling just a few improvements, you'll be laying down the foundations for a process of continuous transformation. So long as these foundations remain anchored in needs and outcomes, you give the change process reason to exist even after the easy fixes have been made. And as your awareness of needs and your ability to anticipate and strategise around them develops, so you build proactivity and anticipation into your organisation – true organisational agility, you might say.

We'll approach this in two ways: firstly through principles, and then by refocusing the tools of chapters 1-4. In Agile terms we're *scaling*, but inviting a *start with what you do now* approach rather than insisting on a framework-based approach.

Five principles of 21ˢᵗ century change leadership

With tongue only slightly in cheek, the stereotypical 20ᵗʰ century change management process might be described as:

1. State a business case

2. Engineer a complex solution

3. Endure a long implementation

4. Live with the consequences: the lingering implementation pain, the debt of missed expectations, and the uncomfortable knowledge that the world has already moved on

Contrast that process with a set of five principles that are much more in keeping with Agendashift's 21st century approach (Figure *35*): *~slow*

Figure 35 The Agendashift principles

Although the correspondence isn't exactly one-to-one, it's not hard to see some resonances between the first four of these Agendashift principles and the first four activities in our facilitation structure of Discovery, Exploration, Mapping, and Elaboration as described in chapters 1-4:

1. **Start with needs** (Discovery) – get a sense of what's needed, based on an appreciation of where we are now and our ambitions for where we'd like to get to

2. **Agree on outcomes** (Exploration) – explore a landscape of obstacles and outcomes, building authentic agreement on outcomes as the basis for change

3. **Keep the agenda for change visible** (Mapping) – use visual mapping to organise, prioritise, cross-check, and communicate

4. **Manage options, testing assumptions** (Elaboration) – generate and select options, frame hypotheses, and develop experiments that will validate or invalidate our assumptions

Continuing in this vein, the fifth principle is about the follow-through:

5. **Organise for clarity, speed, and mutual accountability** (Operation) – organise your experiments and your lines of communication such that:

   o It is clear to all what is happening and why

   o Decisions are made quickly by the right people

   o Transparency and support are both given and received, with responsibility shared both for impact and for how results are achieved

As well as being good principles by which to operate a transformation initiative or even a product development process, they work also as long-lasting principles of continuous transformation. Here they are again, but instead of presenting them imperatively, we present them descriptively in the style of the Agendashift assessment prompts. As with the real prompts, we paint a picture of what it's like to have worked this way for some time, demonstrating that they're more than just one-off activities, phases, or interventions:

1. **Start with needs** – We understand why the organisation should continue to exist, discovering and rediscovering the needs of customers, staff, and the other stakeholders that it must serve

2. **Agree on outcomes** – We maximise potential and minimise friction by deferring and delegating the 'how'; by habit and deliberate practice we focus first on the intent of any change

3. **Keep the agenda for change visible** – We maintain alignment on organisational themes, goals, and priorities, keeping them (and progress against them) visible and under regular review as they evolve

4. **Manage options, testing assumptions** – We make progress by generating and prioritising options, surfacing their assumptions, testing them through experiments, and incorporating learning

5. **Organise for clarity, speed, and mutual accountability –** Our organisation is designed and operated such that decisions about delivery or change can be made quickly and safely, close to where the real action takes place

A change of focus

You could use these principles and their high level prompts as a conversation starter, a way to identify current obstacles and their associated outcomes. We're going to take that idea a little further. To achieve the dual goals of putting this engaging, needs-driven and outcome-oriented continuous transformation into Operation (pun intended) and reinforcing everything we've done up to this point, we're going to take the tools of the preceding chapters and focus them on the organisation's ability to develop, retarget, and reconfigure itself.

In short, the delivery focus of Discovery, Exploration, Mapping, and Elaboration as presented in the preceding chapters will now be replaced by an adaptability focus. The modifications necessary to achieve this are as follows:

1. **Discovery**: Change the content but not the instructions of the *Celebration* exercise and the *Everyone able to work consistently at their best (True North)* exercise. We now want these exercises to help participants imagine what an adaptable organisation could be like, and to relate the benefits of adaptability to the circumstances that the organisation expects, hopes, or fears to find itself in.

2. **Exploration**: Replace the *delivery assessment* (the clue is in the name) with an adaptability assessment. Rather than starting from scratch, we'll do that by modifying the existing one.

And that's it! Mapping and Elaboration come away unscathed because there's nothing particularly delivery-specific about them.

Visualising this change of focus, we're looking at the ability to effect change around process, organisation, and capability, moving from *delivery* and *performance* at the bottom of the triangle figure of Chapter 1 (reproduced here in Figure 36) to *capability* and (in particular) *adaptability* on the right hand side.

Figure 36 The Organisation/Product/Process triangle

Assessing for adaptability (prompts 1-5)

I'll leave the Discovery modifications for the reader – potentially a nice workshop exercise in itself. As for the assessment template modifications, look at what happens to an initial selection of delivery-focussed prompts when words like *'work'* and *'work item'* are replaced with *'change'*. The translation isn't completely mechanical (in the interests of readability I made some tweaks afterwards), but still it's very straightforward:

1.1   Our *change* process and the *changes* currently in progress within it are easily visible to all involved and interested parties

1.2   We have visibility of *changes* due to enter the *change* process soon

3.1   We work with those whose needs we are meeting in order to understand, shape and size potential *changes* before committing to *testing them*

4.2   We incorporate *stakeholder* feedback into our *changes* while they are in the *change*

4.3   We continue to own *changes* until *we have confirmation* that needs are being met

How would you have reworded these prompts? If you find the word *'change'* too ambiguous, you could try words like *'adaptation'* or *'improvement'*. Whatever the words you choose, the point is that in an adaptable organisation, change is treated like real work. It *is* real work, even if your organisation treats it as something curiously voluntary, something that is managed ad hoc, something that happens only at the whim of someone senior, or a job for external consultants.

The ease of this rewording is another demonstration of chapter 4's product/process duality: what works for product (or service) delivery often translates naturally into process improvement, and vice versa. Here, we've taken statements that describe desirable properties of a product (or service) delivery process, and turned them into statements that describe the operation of an effective change process (a change process that enables change rather than suppresses it, in case the phrase has any such connotations).

How well do these reworded prompts describe the basic operation of change in your organisation? Using the four-point scoring scale from Chapter 2, take a few moments to begin an assessment. Here are the first five modified prompts again (we'll revise all 18 over the course of this chapter; these originated in the Transparency, Collaboration, and Customer Focus categories):

1.1 Our *change* process and the *changes* currently in progress within it are easily visible to all involved and interested parties

1.2 We have visibility of *changes* due to enter the *change* process soon

3.1 We work with those whose needs we are meeting in order to understand, shape and size potential *changes* before committing to *testing them*

4.2 We incorporate *stakeholder* feedback into our *changes* while they are in the *change* process

4.3 We continue to own *changes* until *we have confirmation* that needs are being met

Next the debrief (Chapter 2):

- *Who scored 3's and 4's for these prompts? What is it that you appreciate here?* (If you're doing this on your own, think about the kinds of answers that your colleagues might give)

- Who's different to that? What explains the 1's and 2's? What aspects of our change process aren't so effective?

And POWT (Chapter 3):

- Which of these **prompts** represent areas of greatest opportunity?

- What **obstacles** stand in their way?

- ***What would you like to have happen*** – the outcomes behind the obstacles

- **Then what happens?** – more outcomes

Add the outcomes you generate here to your transformation map (Chapter 3) and prioritise them relative to the outcomes represented there already. With practice and a pad of stickies in hand, this whole process can be completed in just a few minutes.

Managing your experiments

In the spirit of chapter 4's *"What has worked elsewhere?"* and *"What would experts from different backgrounds recommend?"* I'm going to describe a Lean Startup-style kanban board (Figure *37*) designed to support the change process:

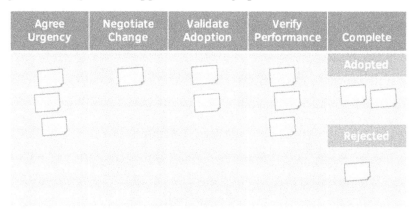

Figure 37 Lean Startup-style kanban board

Each sticky on this board represents a change. In the previous chapter we learned how to frame changes as experiments, so the board could be said to be managing a portfolio of experiments.

Let's take a single sticky's eye view as – over a period of time – it moves across the board from left to right:

- **Agree Urgency**: While here, it is positioned vertically relative to other stickies in some kind of priority order, with the most urgent changes floating to the top. When our sticky's turn comes and there is capacity for it to progress, it moves to **Negotiate change**. If in the meantime it becomes apparent that this progression is not likely to happen within any meaningful timeframe, the sticky moves instead to **Rejected**.

- **Negotiate Change**: Relevant parties (as identified on the change's A3) must now attempt to agree the details of the change that the sticky represents. This negotiation can go one of two ways: if successful, the sticky moves to **Validate**

adoption; otherwise it moves across to **Rejected**, likely signalling either a failure of negotiation or the infeasibility of the change.

- **Validate Adoption**: Does the change work for the people who operate the impacted process? It may take some time to be sure of this, both to iron out any early issues and to be confident that it will stick. A successful conclusion takes the sticky to the next column, **Verify performance**; failure takes it to **Rejected**.

- **Verify Performance**: Are we seeing the impact we hoped for? Again, this might take a while, and again, it's going to go one of two ways, this time to **Adopted** or **Rejected**.

- **Adopted** and **Rejected**: One way or the other, the change is now **Complete** – all decisions have been made, insights have been captured on the A3, and everything is either fully implemented or cleanly rolled back. Let's hope it stays done; after a settling-in period and a final review, the sticky can be removed.

Common to each of the highly-visible decision points in this process is the distinct possibility that stickies will be moved unceremoniously to the **Rejected** column. Every such move represents a clear decision on priorities, the invalidation of an assumption, the rejection of an option, or the "failure" of an experiment, and it's a sign of health that these decisions are being made.

The technical term that is often used to describe this kind of policy framework is *fail fast*. It's a slightly unfortunate term when used in this kind of context, as it sometimes necessitates the rather awkward explanation "there is no failure when there is learning". Avoiding any such embarrassment I sometimes use the less loaded term *reject fast*, emphasising timely and mostly regret-free decision making.

If your existing change process isn't already experiment-based, you might consider introducing a board like this along with its *reject fast* policies. There are two main ways of making this work, and neither of them require you to abandon your existing process until you're completely ready:

1. Use a board to manage the finer detail – the day-to-day experiments – allowing your existing change process to manage things at a larger scale as before

2. Use a board to 'wrap' an existing change process – allowing existing systems to manage the nitty-gritty details whilst framing, developing, and tracking experiments at the higher level

These work at two different levels and they can be used together. Take the first approach if your day-to-day process needs some help. Use the second to track experiments over longer timeframes and to ensure that insights get captured and the learning incorporated.

Swimlanes

The idea of boards working at different levels suggests a couple of ways to manage experiments that involve pilot experiments. Quite feasibly, you could:

1. Use two similar boards, one to manage the higher-level experiments, the other to manage the pilot experiments

2. Use one board but in some way distinguish the different experiment types, perhaps with stickies of contrasting colours

A third and highly practical solution is to group related experiments into horizontal swimlanes. It's as though each multi-experiment outcome or higher-level experiment gets a board of its own (Figure 38):

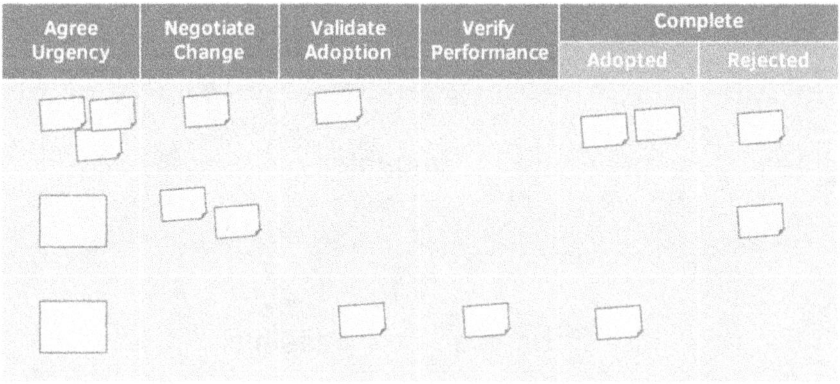

Figure 38 Swimlanes

Here I've drawn the **Adopted** and **Rejected** columns side by side, but that's ok.

Valuable, Feasible, Usable

That Lean Startup-style board design has a nice correspondence to a Venn diagram (Figure 39) that also originates in the Lean Startup community:

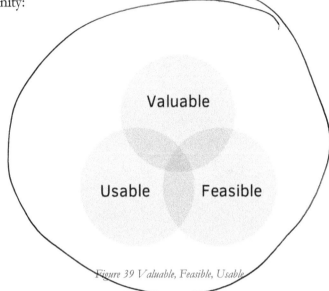

Figure 39 Valuable, Feasible, Usable

It neatly summarises the rationale of each column and of the process overall:

- In **Agree urgency**, we're deciding which change to make next, presumably the one that will be most *valuable* to us (relative to cost, risk, time, and other factors)

- In **Negotiate change** we're digging into the detail, searching for a *feasible* solution that is acceptable to all parties

- In **Validate adoption** we're making sure that the change is *usable*; there is after all no point in pretending to adopt a change that won't stick

- In **Verify performance** we make an evidence-based judgement on whether or not the change really is *valuable*: it's not too late to decide that the change should not be adopted

- In the final column, we know that every item in **Adopted** has passed all those checks (they are all valuable, feasible, and usable); everything else has been **Rejected** (fast), with no lasting harm done

Reviewing the board

Although the stickies move across the board from left to right, experience teaches us to review the board from right to left, fostering a focus on completion:

- Looking at the changes we completed most recently, will they stay completed? Did we remember to capture insights?

- What can we do to get our nearly-completed changes over the line?

- Are there any issues blocking our in-progress changes? What's being done to unblock them? If not blocked, are they progressing as expected?

- Do we have the capacity to start new changes? If that opportunity is coming soon, do we understand which change(s) will be selected next, and why?

For fast progress, review the board frequently. If you already run daily standup meetings and frequent reviews (eg retrospectives) as part of your delivery process, the cost should be negligible.

Pull rather than push (prompts 6-8)

I've adapted another group of prompts, all from the Balance category of the original assessment template. They encourage changes to be pulled rather than pushed through the process:

2.1   We bring *changes* into the *change* process only as capacity allows, preferring to finish *changes* already in progress than to start new *changes*

2.2   We maintain a clear separation between *changes* currently in progress and *changes* still under consideration

2.3   We take steps to avoid being overburdened with more *changes* than we can manage simultaneously

You know the drill: review scores, then prompts, obstacles, outcomes, and more outcomes!

Again, in the spirit of *"What has worked elsewhere?"* and *"What would experts from different backgrounds recommend?"* I will suggest that you consider using more than one of the several standard tools available. You might, for example, implement Scrum-style sprint planning and timeboxing in conjunction with Kanban's explicit limits on work-in-progress. This might seem redundant, but the more ways you can find to keep your workload under control, the less that any single control mechanism will come to be seen as a source of conflict.

There are some specific benefits to be gained when the number of active experiments is limited appropriately. With fewer experiments running in parallel it's much easier to isolate their impact, making it easier to work out which change caused which effect. Fewer experiments also means less risk of confusion, for example making it less likely that people will do the wrong thing due to uncertainty over what version of the official process now applies.

Within sensible bounds, having fewer experiments in progress doesn't mean that less gets done; rather it helps to get them completed quickly. Definitively finishing experiments creates capacity for further experimentation based on new knowledge, and the learning process continues. Counterintuitive as it may seem, less really is more!

Let it flow (prompts 9-12)

Whilst balance is certainly vital to flow, it is not sufficient. These prompts focus attention directly on the flow of changes through the change process:

1.3   We can see which *changes* are blocked and for what reason

5.1   We can predict with reasonable confidence how long it will take to deliver *changes* of typical value and risk

5.2   We understand the performance of our *change process* in sufficient detail to make timely decisions, to set appropriate expectations, and to focus our *efforts to improve it*

5.3   We proactively identify and address dependencies and other impediments to *the flow of changes through our change process*

Once more: review scores, then prompts, obstacles, outcomes, and more outcomes.

Blockers and dependencies are a particularly pernicious problem in change management. Often we're trying to effect change in areas beyond our control, and because we're deliberately keeping the number of in-progress experiments under careful control, any delay will have a disproportionate impact on our active portfolio.

Two sayings apply: *"Prevention is better than cure"*, and *"Don't start what you can't finish"*. You'll find that your experiments flow better when they're small enough that the nasties have little room in which to hide (pilot experiments are your friend). Sequence your changes sensibly, and take every opportunity to discuss them, even before the formal negotiations begin. If you really must start work on changes known to have unresolved dependencies, keep those dependencies highly visible. Manage them actively enough and you might be fortunate enough to get everything to land at just the right time.

If, despite all your skills of prevention and anticipation you do get bitten, here's a great pattern I learned from my friends at Odigeo in Barcelona. They call it the *'holding pattern'* and it works as follows:

• When an item gets blocked, they flag it so that everyone knows about it and it is sure to be discussed in every standup meeting until it is resolved. Everyone understands that resolving blockers is a high priority activity.

• For a defined period (a few days), blocked items remain in place on the kanban board. Importantly, they count against the board's capacity so that no-one will be tempted just to ignore the problem and start something else. Be in no doubt: resolving blockers is a high priority activity!

- After that initial period, the item gets moved to a holding area, freeing capacity for other work. The team still discusses its status and any progress each day.

- If the blocker does get resolved, the item moves to the front of the board's input queue. It will be the first item to get pulled into the main process as soon as capacity becomes available. Rationale: It is better to finish something that has already been started than to start something new!

- If the item remains stuck in the holding area for too long (*'too long'* being a period defined in team policy), it is either returned to the backlog to be reprioritised at some later date, or abandoned altogether.

Towards continuous transformation (prompts 13-18)

Even after adaptation, none of the mini assessment's prompts quite boil down to *"We embrace a process of continuous transformation"*. That said, prompt 6.1 below (the fourth one down) comes pretty close, and all of the remaining prompts of the 18 support that idea:

3.2 Our *change* process encourages collaboration across roles and specialties

3.3 We meet on a regular basis to review *our change process and its effectiveness*

4.1 We seek to align our *changes* to shared goals, prioritising for maximum impact

6.1 Together, we strive to meet customer needs, improve our *change processes*, and develop new capabilities; in all three pursuits we are appropriately recognised, supported, and rewarded

6.2 We ensure that opportunities for improvement are recognised and systematically followed through

6.3 We all share the responsibility to seek clarification, to highlight problems, and to come up with improvement ideas

In fact, they all work remarkably well even without modification:

3.2 Our delivery process encourages collaboration across roles and specialties

3.3 We meet on a regular basis to review and improve our outputs and processes

4.1 We seek to align our work to shared goals, prioritising for maximum impact

6.1 Together, we strive to meet customer needs, improve our delivery systems, and develop new capabilities; in all three pursuits we are appropriately recognised, supported, and rewarded

6.2 We ensure that opportunities for improvement are recognised and systematically followed through

6.3 We all share the responsibility to seek clarification, to highlight problems, and to come up with improvement ideas

Together, they paint a picture of alignment pursued through collaboration and mutual accountability both across the organisation and vertically. Fantastic when you have it, but what if you don't? I'm not going to pretend that there are easy solutions that can be implemented overnight, but behind several of these prompts is a simple concept – the *feedback loop* – that has a critical part to play. If you want your organisation to change, you must understand its feedback loops!

Feedback loops

When I use the phrase *'feedback loops'* I typically mean something like this:

Regular opportunities to bring people and information together for the purpose of making decisions

In the glossary of *Kanban from the Inside* I was more careful:

For the most part, [feedback loops] refers to the deliberate incorporation of feedback in the design of a process so that the resulting product, service, or the delivery process itself can be controlled and improved. Note, however, that not all feedback loops are there by design; some may be hard to identify, and they are not always benign.

Do not doubt the power of feedback loops. Here are some examples of feedback loops "gone bad":

- **Requirements review**: Projects over-specified – too big and with solutions over-constrained – because:

  i.   The system expects every possible objection to be anticipated and addressed up front

  ii. Customers have little expectation of timely delivery and feel forced to 'kitchen sink' their requests

- **Project planning**: Projects planned with big-bang deliveries, on the (usually flawed) assumptions that needs will be met without further iteration and that incremental models of delivery will be less efficient.

- **Project approval**: Projects approved without regard to delivery capacity, approved instead on their individual merits or for reasons of politics or vanity. The resulting competition for resources inflicts serious delay and frustration on customers and delivery teams alike.

- **Progress reviews**: Increasing numbers of features built but not tested or nor validated – and this inventory of perhaps un-needed work celebrated as evidence of positive progress and an asset to the organisation.

- **Operations reviews**: High staff utilisation rates (high *resource efficiency*) celebrated, despite long delays to customers (poor *flow efficiency*); the invisible accumulation of *technical debt*; and never mind the human cost! Under these conditions, customer responsiveness can be addressed only by working harder or making short-term compromises on quality, compounding issues of sustainability and risking a downward spiral from which recovery will be even more difficult.

- **Post-project reviews**: Cost and due date conformance celebrated despite repeated re-planning, unhappy customers, and no "lessons learned" actually put into practice.

I've seen each of those issues multiple times. Some common root causes:

- Basic failings – a lack of will or competence in prioritisation, planning, or the conduct of meetings, for example

- Celebrating the wrong things to excess, institutionalising poor choices of values and behaviours

- Making decisions in forums too far removed from where the competence lies or the impact will be felt

- Lack of consideration for activity and priorities elsewhere

- Broken relationships, for example between the organisation and its customers, and between the organisation and its staff

Ironically, many of these problems are caused by the very same mechanisms that were supposed to prevent them. "Doing it properly" (by their understanding of 20th century standards, at least) made things worse, not better. Moreover, the system tends to promote the people most responsible! This isn't malevolence, it's just how systems tend to work if there aren't mechanisms in place to prevent it.

Fortunately, all is not lost. Consider this model for feedback loops (Figure *40*) by my friend and former colleague David J. Anderson. The terminology here comes from Kanban, but regardless of the actual delivery model employed – and including delivery models well outside of Lean-Agile – it's a really helpful way of understanding what's going on and identifying key activities missing from your organisational design.

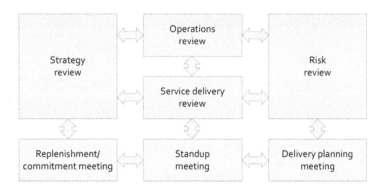

Figure 40 Feedback loops (based on The Kanban Cadences, David J. Anderson)

Along the bottom of this picture we have the delivery process:

- **Replenishment/commitment meeting**: Whatever it happens to be called in practice, this is the place for deciding what to work on in the coming days or weeks, coherent (one hopes) with both strategy and the state of work already in progress. In Scrum, for example, this meeting takes the form of the Sprint Planning meeting, in which the *sprint backlog* for the next *sprint* (a timebox) is populated with work taken from the *product backlog*.

- **Standup meeting**: A meeting held frequently (typically daily), in which progress, issues, and next steps are discussed. Often known as the 'daily standup' or the 'daily scrum' (from which Scrum gets its name, by analogy with the sport of Rugby). In Kanban, much of this meeting is spent reviewing the board (from right to left, as we'll see later).

- **Delivery planning meeting**: A meeting (or equivalent activity) in which it is decided what will be delivered out of the process and onwards to (or at least towards) the customer. These customer deliveries might be planned before work starts (in Scrum via a combination of *Release Planning* and *Sprint Planning*), planned opportunistically as work nears completion, or achieved near-seamlessly with the help of automation (*continuous delivery*).

The details (and even the decision-making sequence) vary, but most delivery processes have these three elements in some form or other. What Lean, Agile, and Lean-Agile processes have in common are the existence (if not the same details) of mechanisms designed to keep workload and capacity in balance, and to incorporate customer feedback into the process. Ideally, that customer feedback is already happening by the replenishment stage – with the customer represented in planning discussions – and continues throughout the process.

Up through the middle of David's model is the skeleton of what might be called an alignment process implemented through connected review meetings with overlapping participation:

- **Standup Meeting**: Primarily for the delivery team, this meeting provides frequent opportunities to review blockers, and to raise concerns and improvement ideas for later exploration. It is also an opportunity to share feedback, insights, and decisions from outside the team.

- **Service Delivery Review**: This meeting provides a regular opportunity to step back from the delivery process and evaluate it thoroughly from multiple perspectives. The formats of these meetings vary; I recommend this "outside-in" (customer-first) agenda:

  o The customer – through direct participation or indirectly via user research, customer support, and so on

  o The organisation – typically via senior members of staff

  o The product – from the product manager, for example

  o The technology platform – eg from technical support

  o The delivery process – eg from a senior engineer and/or delivery manager, or the delivery team representing themselves directly

  o The delivery pipeline – eg from the product manager and/or delivery manager

- **Operations Review**: This is rarely implemented as a single meeting, but logically it's the home of the big decisions about investment, organisation, and capability. It works to longer time horizons than the (possibly multiple) Service Delivery Reviews that fall under its purview, so its meetings need not be so frequent.

Operated well and with the right participation, this alignment process reinforces mutual transparency and accountability. It helps to maintain strategic coherence, and it both informs and is informed by the organisation's current risk profile and risk appetite.

In times of change, the Service Delivery Review and other similarly-structured capability reviews are particularly useful for their ability to connect new processes to the old organisation. When the delivery team is proactive in setting it up they create the opportunity to structure the meeting, to offer metrics more consistent with new values, and to set the tone. With the participation of the right senior staff (for the second item on the agenda, not the first!), reviews like this can be pivotal. The outside-in (customer-first) agenda I suggest above maximises the alignment opportunity; a right-to-left (kanban style) approach to the in-progress work helps to keep things moving towards completion. When they happen regularly with the right people in the room and clear evidence of progress from meeting to meeting, participants feel encouraged, accountable, and supported by the organisation.

Do Agile processes include this kind of alignment process? They can, but many unfortunately don't, at least not very completely. Scrum, the leading Agile process framework, contains the opportunity to cover Service Delivery Review across its Sprint Review and Retrospective meetings, but often these meetings lack the range, the rigour, the organisational support, and the follow-through. Scrum's intention to protect teams from management may be laudable, but the end result can be a loss to both sides. Just as the Lean movement discovered through the 1990's (see the **Toyota Kata** section at the end of Chapter 4), it is hard to sustain change. It's harder still when you insist carrying the burden on your own.

Where to start?

Agendashift as Lean-Agile process

Let's recap:

1. **Discovery** – articulating something about where we'd like to get to, based on current and future needs

2. **Exploration** – identifying opportunities for positive change, based on a more detailed understanding of where we are

3. **Mapping** – visualising our plans and priorities, reviewing strategy

4. **Elaboration** – generating, framing, and developing actions, testing our thinking

5. **Operation** – learning to treat change as real work, embedding the transformation process

You might still be thinking *"Plenty of plausible-sounding words there, but what makes this process Lean, Agile, or Lean-Agile?"*. It's a fair question – there are enough linear, top down, cookie-cutter, imposed, consultant-knows-best, and resistance-trumping models out there already and we surely don't need yet another one like that! Can we demonstrate that it embodies collaboration, iteration, flow, pull, feedback and so on?

We'll use an old Lean trick: review the process backwards, from finish to start, right to left. It might seem an odd thing to do, but it's helpful in two important ways:

1. It helps us ensure that each activity pulls just the right inputs from its predecessors and produces no un-needed outputs
2. It helps us understand the rhythms and level of effort required to keep work flowing smoothly to completion

So from 5. Operation, down to 1. Discovery:

5. Operation

We meet frequently to review the changes we have in progress and to share what insights we've gathered along the way. We're validating the impact of our most advanced experiments to help us decide whether or not to adopt them formally. Some of our other experiments haven't reached that stage yet – either we're making sure of their usability (there's no point in endorsing changes that won't stick), or we're still establishing their feasibility. Further upstream, we keep a small backlog of prioritised, appropriately-sequenced, and well-understood changes that we'll begin as capacity permits.

Although the scope of our process is well defined, we don't do this work in isolation. From our side, we're transparent about what we're doing and how we're performing from a range of perspectives (starting with the perspective of our customers). In return, we can expect strong support when the changes we need to make aren't entirely within our span of control or when we're asked to do things that we haven't done before.

4. Elaboration

We're careful not to specify changes until we're close to needing that level of detail – this isn't *big design up front* (BDUF) but a *just-in-time* (JIT) process. By deferring design choices until the best possible moment we give ourselves the opportunity to incorporate feedback from previous experiments (successful changes or otherwise) and to take into account any recent environmental changes that may have taken place outside our control.

Where appropriate (which is much of the time), we take a hypothesis-driven approach. In the pursuit of the highest priority outcomes on our transformation map we generate options, form hypotheses, identify who should to be involved, design pilot experiments to test our assumptions, and plan to capture insights.

3. Mapping

There is much that we'd like to do and it's important to keep our ideas organised. Call it a planning tool if you like, we use a *transformation map*, analogous to a *story map*, except that the elements being organised aren't features, user stories, or job stories, but outcomes.

We prioritise outcomes within categories before looking across categories and deciding what we will work on next. In setting priorities overall, we may choose to give special emphasis to a particular category for a while, or decide instead that it's better to choose a minimal set of independent or complementary outcomes from across the board.

From time to time we refresh the map. Either in conjunction with a new round of Exploration or as a standalone activity, we reflect on current obstacles and map out the desired outcomes that lie behind them.

2. Exploration

Exploration keeps the transformation map both anchored in reality and connected with the vision, the output from Discovery.

Exploration is a generative process. Informed by the results from the assessment tool, we collaborate on identifying areas of opportunity and their respective obstacles, then 'flip' those obstacles into the outcomes that will become either the work items or the organising themes on our transformation map.

We do enough of this up front to prime the pump and to get a good sense of what it is we're really dealing with. We revisit it periodically: as our transformation progresses, so too will our understanding of what's urgent, what's possible, and where we think we're headed.

1. Discovery

What would it be like if everyone were able to work at their best, individually, within teams, and across teams? What if we could have the right conversations between the right people always happening at the best possible moment? What if needs were anticipated and met at just the right time too? Imagine that!

Agendashift as coaching framework

Agendashift-as-Lean-Agile-process describes one possible realisation of continuous transformation. Of course most of us aren't there yet, so how might we structure our initial approach? A coach might describe something along these lines:

1. Work with the client or sponsor to identify the strategic goals and needs that the engagement must address, setting the right tone in terms of ambition without losing sight of where the real challenges and opportunities lie

2. Explore key areas of opportunity with the client in more detail, identifying obstacles, and from those generate a set of outcomes that represent the scope, objectives, and priorities of the engagement

3. Help the client to understand the challenge in enough breadth to ensure that nothing important gets missed, and with depth sufficient to keep the coaching process fed with fresh and important challenges to investigate

4. Drawing on a range of models, tools, and frameworks, encourage the client to generate and develop options for concrete action

5. Through appropriate transparency, mutual accountability, and feedback in the coaching relationship with the client, ensure both the follow-through on actions already agreed and the flow of new ideas that can actioned as capacity becomes available

Thinly disguised, this is of course our 5-step activity flow and the 5 principles again.

With the exception perhaps of step 1 (Discovery), this is a pretty accurate description of how Agendashift was applied by its earliest adopters. Formally, the Discovery part was the last to be developed, even if any sensible engagement model must at some level begin with conversations such as these.

In those early days, the Operation part relied on whatever change process happened to exist already in our client organisations. Each organisation had evolved its own unique way of doing things, but nevertheless they would have had little difficulty in recognising many of the techniques described in this chapter. Later, the adaptability assessment was developed as a non-prescriptive way to help organisations explore this part of the landscape more thoroughly.

Typically, an initial pass was either completed in a single session of 1-2 days or spread across multiple encounters with individuals or teams over a period of weeks. These two patterns still apply today: whilst intense and comprehensive workshops remain a key offering of my own business, many partners prefer to use the tools and materials piecemeal over an extended period and I'd be the first to recognise that this is often the more sustainable approach.

Groundwork

Not ready yet for a coordinated effort? There is still plenty of preparatory work you can do. Each chapter includes some reflective tools you can try on your own even if you're not ready to facilitate them (or have them facilitated) for others.

You can develop your appreciation for the feedback loops that operate in your organisation. Not just the formal feedback loops that are there by design, but the vicious and virtuous circles that drive behaviours that aren't so easy to explain. What gets measured? What gets celebrated? Who gets rewarded? What does that say about the real values of your organisation? If you could cause some different things to receive their proper recognition, what would they be?

Armed with answers to those questions, you will begin to understand what it takes to operate a truly responsive and adaptive organisation, and perhaps along the way generate more empathy for the individuals involved too. As your awareness of feedback loops grows, it becomes easier to put aside automatic (and likely flawed) assumptions of bad motives when you see unhelpful behaviours.

More practically, you can take a look at your review meetings – service delivery reviews, capability reviews, strategy reviews, even standup meetings and planning meetings – in whatever form they currently take. In the spirit of *start with what you do now*, here are three dimensions in which most such meetings can be improved:

1. How might they be more outside-in? Who would best represent each agenda item? In what order? Sharing what metrics (and implying what values)? What contradictions are likely to be found between these different perspectives, and how might they be dealt with?

2. How might they be more right-to-left? Do participants feel mutually accountable for an end-to-end process that focusses on realising outcomes and finishes with validation? What keeps those outcomes connected to authentic needs, and how are needs discovered and prioritised? What keeps workloads at appropriate levels, in balance with capacity?

3. Horizontally and vertically, do your meetings together cover the organisation (or at least the part that is the focus of your interest)? Horizontally, does each contributing part feel sufficiently connected, with overlapping participation across meetings? Vertically, is the organisation adequately represented so that delivery work, capability-related work, and mission can be kept in alignment? See *Figure 41*, the inverted pyramid, Agendashift-style.

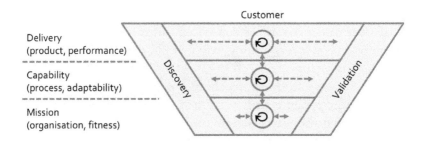

Figure 41 The inverted pyramid, Agendashift-style

You can make a start with some even more fundamental questions:

*   What are our goals?

*   What obstacles stand in our way?

- What would we like to have happen?

- Then what happens?

It's a pattern repeated many times in this book. Clean conversations that help model the challenge and invite ambitions to be articulated and agreed, the basis for coherent, outcome-oriented collaboration on a range of potential solutions, with buy-in already established. Whether or not you are ready for continuous transformation, isn't that a good place to start?

Behind the scenes

A process of culture formation

In *Kanban from the Inside* I made one glaring omission: there is no reference to Edgar Schein. Some reviewers were of the opinion that any book that takes an explicitly values-based approach to culture must surely make reference to his work. I'm only too happy to fix that now.

His writings on values are indeed important, but I want to highlight something else: the beautifully simple observation that *culture formation* is a process. This is both bad news and good news:

- Culture can't be wished, designed, or ordered into being; you can't hope to control all the individual experiences that combine to influence culture over time.

- You can however make the culture formation process more visible and better informed. You can cause organisational assumptions to be challenged and perhaps 'disconfirmed', *disconfirmation* being the uncomfortable but powerful precursor to *unlearning* and then new learning. Better still, you incorporate regular challenge into the organisation's management systems so that this learning process is sustained.

Make that a participatory process, and you go a long way to describing Agendashift. Here is Schein on turnarounds:

"Turnarounds usually require the involvement of all organization members, so that the dysfunctional elements of the present culture become clearly visible to everyone. The process of developing new assumptions involves defining new values and goals through teaching, coaching, changing the structure and processes where necessary; consistently paying attention to and rewarding evidence of learning new ways".

That's from this must-read:

- *Organizational Culture and Leadership*
  Edgar H. Schein (5th edition, 2016, Jossey-Bass)

Most of the time we won't want the sense of crisis or coercion that goes with turnarounds (and inauthentic crisis typically has the opposite effect to the one desired). But amend the beginning of that quote to read *"Continuous transformation requires..."* and I could hardly have put it better myself.

In another highly recommended book, Peter Block further emphasises the need for genuine participation:

"Results are achieved when members of a system collectively choose to move in a certain direction. It is this act of choice that is critical. ... No change – no matter how wise and needed – will help if there is not a widespread and deep sense that each individual exercising choice and working together must make this work."

Source:

- *Flawless Consulting*
  Peter Block (3rd edition, 2011, John Wiley & Sons)

Scrumban and Lean Startup

Towards the start of this chapter I described the use of kanban systems to manage experiments inside and/or wrapped around an existing change process. Thanks to product/process duality, I was of course at the same time describing a technique that works well for delivery processes also.

When the core delivery process is (or starts out as) Scrum, this essentially describes Scrumban. This is the use of Kanban (the method as much as the boards) inside and/or outside Scrum, to help manage the detail, to help manage long-lived experiments, and to encourage the process to evolve in the direction of fast and smooth flow.

I've worked as delivery manager on two UK government digital projects and consultant to a couple of others, an experience I like to describe as "surprisingly awesome". Those aren't words you would have associated with government projects in the past, but to see these very 21st century ideas adopted in the government sector with such commitment has been inspiring.

Both of the projects that I served as delivery manager started with a Scrum-based process and both succeeded in evolving their processes rapidly over a period of months. In their early days, both projects appreciated the focus of the *"potentially shippable increment"* (a Scrum concept that definitely has its place, even if I don't much care for it as a goal). Later on, both projects became capable of real and reliable (not merely 'potential') production deployments as soon as they had something of value to deliver and lead times for new features dropped rapidly.

One of those projects, *Carer's Allowance* at the Department for Work and Pensions (DWP), wrapped the delivery process in a very recognisable Lean Startup process. It was successful too: *"Unquestionably excellent"* was *Computer Weekly*'s verdict! *Find an apprenticeship* at the Skills Funding Agency (SFA), placed a strong emphasis on rapid cycles of prototyping and user testing. Sometimes we would see multiple ideas tested on volunteer users (citizens, not staff) in the course of a single evening's lab session.

Start with needs

As well as of course to the teams involved, significant credit for the successes of those projects should rightly be attributed to the boldness of the UK government's digital strategy. Through Government Digital Services (GDS, a part of the Cabinet Office), it set out to transform government departments and agencies on the back of digital projects.

"Start with needs" (Agendashift principle #1) is inspired by the first and best known of GDS's design principles, officially worded as *"Start with user needs"* and sometimes presented as *"Start with needs – user needs, not government needs"*. See:

- *Government Digital Service Design Principles*
  www.gov.uk/design-principles

I would rank GDS's successes as follows:

1. First and foremost, they have succeeded in turning user needs (as opposed to government needs) into a strategic value. Any project unable to demonstrate a long-term organisational commitment to meeting changing needs carries a very real risk of public failure. As a result, teams have learned to explore needs and to iterate on user experience (UX) and solution design with an intensity that would put most private sector projects to shame.

2. Individual projects, groups of projects, and communities of practice across government became fertile environments for innovation and learning. GDS communicated clear expectations around agility but took care not to prescribe any particular Agile process framework, instead encouraging each team to evolve processes that would work for them and to share their experiences with others.

3. Multiple demonstrations of digital services neither as supplier-dominated, fixed term projects nor as isolated bubbles of Agile culture, instead as bridgeheads that continue to influence how government services as a whole will be delivered. Progress here has been achieved through a combination of policy changes (eg

in supplier management) and that strategic commitment to needs.

And that's just the organisational impact. It is widely recognised that the digital services delivered this way have been of high quality from the perspective of the service user, making government services in the UK much more accessible than previously, even to the most vulnerable of citizens. That all of this has been achieved in times of austerity seems remarkable.

I should mention that the innovation and learning of point 2 above wasn't only achieved through the avoidance of prescription – it was the product also of some deliberate organisational design. I first met Emily Webber when she was Head of Agile Delivery at GDS, and she described her role as being about building professional communities, more specifically the kind of communities where learning would flourish. She has since written a book on the subject:

* *Building Successful Communities of Practice: Discover How Connecting People Makes Better Organisations*
  Emily Webber (2016, Tacit)

See also Chapter 3, The needs behind the stories.

Feedback loops, leadership, and Systems Thinking

In *Kanban from the Inside* I approached feedback loops from two different angles:

1. In a chapter on Transparency (the first of nine values), looking at the regular ceremonies and reporting structures that support the delivery process and stimulate evolutionary change

2. Under a heading of Systems Thinking, looking more generally at *reinforcing loops, balancing loops, vicious circles,* and *virtuous circles –* feedback loops that can be hard to identify but can do much to explain why things are the way they are

A very different kind of book is *Turn the ship around!* by former submarine captain L. David Marquet. Through his story, Marquet describes *"pushing authority* [downwards] *to the information"*, a *leader-leader* model of mutual accountability, the means by which a very real transfer of authority is effected. Marquet had come to the realisation that the design of feedback loops says much about the organisation's – in this case the US Navy's – true attitude to leadership. If you really want effective leadership at every level, it's not enough just to call for it: you must design for it. The book is a must-read (or a must-listen – I recommend the audiobook wholeheartedly):

- *Turn the Ship Around!: A True Story of Turning Followers into Leaders* L. David Marquet (2013, Portfolio)

Systems Dynamics is a branch of Systems Thinking that has much to say about feedback loops. A superb book on Systems Thinking from a leading member of this school is by the late Donella ("Dana") Meadows:

- *Thinking in Systems: A Primer* Donnella Meadows (2008, White River Junction)

I also recommend John Gall, who manages to be both insightful and highly entertaining at the same time:

- *Systemantics: How Systems Work & Especially How They Fail* John Gall (1977, Quadrangle/New York Times Book Co)

Gall is known for his law:

A complex system that works is invariably found to have evolved from a simple system that worked. A complex system designed from scratch never works and cannot be patched up to make it work. You have to start over with a working simple system.

So to finish:

- Start with what you do now [not with complex solutions designed from scratch]
- Begin [to change] with the end in mind

Key points – 5. Operation

Concepts and tools:

- From the 20th century to the 21st:

    o   Justifications, requirements, preconceived designs, and top-down change management versus a continuous process of transformation centered on needs and outcomes

    o   A 20th century sense of "doing it properly", its flawed assumptions, and its unfortunate consequences versus true business agility

    o   21st century principles of change leadership

- Treating change as "real work":

    o   Adaptability as an issue of core organisational process, not just speed of delivery

    o   The adaptability assessment

    o   Continuous transformation sustained by the organisation's own systems

- Tools for managing experiments

- Feedback loops, benign and otherwise

- Service Delivery Reviews and other capability reviews – outside-in and right-to-left

- Covering the inverted pyramid, connecting both horizontally and top (customer facing) to bottom (most senior)

- Agendashift as:

    o   A model for Lean-Agile processs

    o   A coaching framework

- Sources of inspiration:

    o   Culture and leadership (Schein, Marquet)

- o *Start with needs* (UK Government Digital Services)
- o Systems Thinking (Meadows, Gall)

Epilogue: The Full Circle exercise

In the style of an Agendashift prompt, compose some sentences that will become "more true" in your organisation as your key outcomes are achieved.

To help you, here are some familiar examples:

- "We identify dependencies between work items in good time and sequence them accordingly"

- "Our vision and purpose are clear to us, our customers, and our stakeholders"

- "We ensure that opportunities for improvement are recognised and systematically followed through"

Style guide:

- **Inclusive** – Start each sentence with "We" or "our" and make it a statement that you believe most of your colleagues could embrace

- **Present tense** – not impossibly out of reach; perhaps there are pockets of this happening already

- **Non-prescriptive** – avoid specifying practices or other means by which this outcome will be achieved, instead allow multiple approaches

Not that they necessarily should, but do your sentences align with any of the six values of the assessment (Transparency, Balance, Collaboration, Flow, Customer focus, Leadership)? If you can see no obvious alignment, do they instead suggest other values? Do these values suggest other sentences that need to be written, covered neither by the original prompts nor yours?

Now, for each of your new 'prompts':

- What obstacles stand in the way of this being realised more fully?
- What would you like to have happen
- Then what happens?

Resources

Resources mentioned in this book

Available via www.agendashift.com/resources:

- Cue cards for the 15-minute FOTO game (Chapter 1)
- Trial access to the mini editions of the Agendashift delivery and adaptability assessments (Chapters 2 and 5 respectively)
- The white paper 6+1 Essential strategies for successful Lean-Agile transformation (Chapter 3)
- The Agendashift A3 template (Chapter 4)
- The Agendashift poster (Introduction), True North (Chapter 1) and Principles (Chapter 5)

The Agendashift partner programme

For a modest annual subscription, Agendashift partners receive:

- A license to use our latest workshop materials, customisable according to need
- The ability to conduct surveys of unlimited size using the full range of templates, including the original 43-prompt delivery assessment (see Chapter 2 for the 18-prompt mini edition), the corresponding pathway template (Chapter 3), and the (still mini-sized) adaptability assessment of Chapter 5.
- An optional listing in the Agendashift partner directory www.agendashift.com/partners
- Onboarding and group calls by video
- Discounts on public workshops
- Access to a private, partner-only Slack channel

For further information, go to www.agendashift.com/partner.

Other resources

- Our Slack community: request your invite via www.agendashift.com/slack

- Our LinkedIn group: www.agendashift.com/linkedin

- Featureban: As used by trainers and coaches in Lean, Agile, and Kanban-related events the world over, Featureban is a simple, fun, and highly customisable Kanban simulation game. Published under a Creative Commons Attribution-ShareAlike 4.0 International license. www.agendashift.com/featureban

- Changeban: a Lean Startup-inspired derivative of Featureban, similarly licensed. www.agendashift.com/changeban

Acknowledgements

It's hard to separate the people who made direct contributions to this book from those who helped me launch and develop Agendashift as a whole. The overlap is great enough that I include names from both categories and in roughly the chronological order of their involvement.

An international effort from the outset, crucial in those earliest days were Dragan Jojic (UK), and Matt Philip (US), then Jussi Mäkelä (Sweden), Patrick Steyaert (Belgium), Olivier My (France), Martien van Steenbergen (Holland), Karl Scotland (UK), Kenny Grant (UK), and Andrea Chiou (US).

Later: Susanne Bartel (Germany), Thorbjørn Sigberg (Norway), Mike Leber (Austria), Brad Hughes (US), Marcus Andrezak (Germany), Kert Petersen (US), Derek Winter (Australia), Richard Cornelius (UK), Joey Spooner (US), Peter Kerschbaumer (Spain), Ray Edgar (UK), Tony Richards (UK), Craig Cockburn (UK), Kevin Murray (UK), Paul Cooper (UK), Liz Keogh (UK), Greg Brougham (UK), John Clapham (UK), Philippe Guenet (UK), Dieter Strasser (Austria), Steven Mackenzie (UK), Allan Kelly (UK), Johan Nordin (Sweden), Rod Sherwin (Australia), Andrew Kidd (UK).

Of those, let me single out four key contributors. Dragan's early work on the assessment prompts was essential to their breadth, their usability, and their impact. Karl helped to push Agendashift upstream, suggesting (and bravely testing) ways to develop the Discovery tools and to integrate the Cynefin exercise more cleanly. Andrea played a key role in the integration of Clean Language, and I'm grateful that through her I have been introduced to Judy Rees and Caitlin Walker, both leading members of the Clean Language community in the UK (Judy and Caitlin are respectively co-author and author of two of the books I recommend in chapter 1). Steven diligently reviewed multiple revisions of this book and pushed me hard to make it what it is today.

I'm grateful to Dave Snowden for the Cynefin four points contextualisation exercise in chapter 2, and to David J. Anderson for permission to reproduce his feedback loops model. A special mention also to Ajay Reddy, who kindly sponsored some work on Servant Leadership. Unknown to either of us the time this came to provide a valuable cross-check to Agendashift.

I must mention my wife Sharon, and not just as a matter of courtesy. This period saw more than our fair share of family crises, stresses, and sadnesses – to the degree that travel (and therefore work) was for long stretches very difficult – but her determination throughout to help create space for this project has been nothing short of inspirational. There were moments of joy to celebrate too, not least our 30th wedding anniversary and the adoption of our long-term foster daughter, Florence. Much of my writing was done from the sofa in Florence's room; I might not have enjoyed getting up in the early hours to attend to Florence's various and complex needs, but I was at least able to put my wakefulness to good use!

Follow the Agendashift blog (blog.agendshift.com) or join us in Slack (www.agendashift.com/slack) or LinkedIn (www.agendashift.com/linkedin) to keep up with and participate in Agendashift-related developments. If you have feedback, a relevant case study, or would like to get in touch for any other reason you can reach me at mike@agendashift.com.

Mike Burrows
February 2018, Chesterfield, UK

About the Author

Mike is known to the Agile and Lean-Agile communities as the author of *Kanban from the Inside* (Blue Hole Press, 2014), the creator of the Featureban simulation game, a keynote speaker at conferences around the world, and as a consultant, coach, and trainer.

Prior to founding Agendashift he was an Executive Director and global development manager for a top-tier investment bank, CTO for a late-stage startup, and (as an associate of Valtech UK) the interim delivery manager for two UK government digital 'exemplar' projects. Before and sometimes during those, a software developer (programming remains a passion).

In 2009 Mike moved with his family from the London commuter belt to the picturesque Derbyshire village of Matlock Bath on the edge of the Peak District, the UK's first National Park. He now lives a few miles further north in the town of Chesterfield with wife Sharon and daughter Florence. They have two grown-up sons, Matthew and Simon.

Index

1-2-4-All (facilitation pattern), 59, 91
15-minute FOTO (coaching game), 15
  cue card, 20, 28, 43, 44, 151
15-Minute FOTO (coaching game), 42
5W (Who, what, when, where, why), 11
6 leadership strategies (model), 78, 151
A3, 93, 96, 107, 121
  Agendashift A3 template, 96, 104, 151
accountability, 53, 134
  mutual, 8, 78, 79, 114, 129, 134, 138, 140, 146
  Organise for clarity, speed, and mutual accountability (principle), 8, 114, 115
action, 6, 83, 86, 135
  areas, 21, 42
  assigned, 111
  ideas, 91, 138
adaptability, 7, 115, 139
Adzic, Gojko, 83
agenda, 140
  customer-first, 133, 134
  Keep the agenda for change visible (principle), 7, 113, 114
Agendashift, 25, 107, 108, 141, 149
  A3 template, 96, 104, 151
  activity flow, 6, 138
  as coaching framework, 138
  as Lean-Agile process, 135
  assessments, 7, 32, 57, 86, 114, 115, 137, 139, 149, 151
  assessments, 151
  principles, 7, 112, 138
  resources, 28, 58, 78, 96, 151
  True North, 7, 25, 115, 151
Agile, 3, 5, 82, 133, 134, 135, 152
  culture bubbles, 144
  frameworks, 2, 4, 26, 69, 134, 144
  manifesto, 23, 25, 26
  principles, 26

transformation, 4
Agree on outcomes (principle), 7, 113, 114
agreement, 2, 3, 21, 39, 120, 124, 141
  Agree on outcomes (principle), 7, 113, 114
  on opportunities, 41
Agreement, 42
  action areas, 42
  facilitation, 42
alignment, 34, 63, 71, 75, 86, 114, 129, 134, 140, 149
  mechanisms, 23, 79
  process, 133, 134
ambitions, 2, 3, 5, 21, 56, 77, 78, 113, 138, 141
Anderson, David J., 81
anticipation, 1, 6, 78, 112, 127
  needs, 1, 6, 7, 14, 78, 112, 137
Appreciative Enquiry, 107
artefacts, 69, 78, 98, 107
aspirations, 3, 21, 84
assessments. *See* Agendashift assessments
assumptions, 27, 97
  developing, 142
  flawed, 130, 139
  Manage options, testing assumptions (principle), 8, 113, 114
  testing, 55, 71, 98, 99, 113, 114, 136
attitudes, 72
authentic situation of need, 83, 140
authenticity, 50, 113, 142
backlog, 128, 132, 136
balance, 126, 133, 140
Balance, 33, 37, 69, 125, 149
  demand and capability, 68, 72, 81
baseline, 99
Beck, Kent, 82
Begin with the end in mind (Covey), 1, 146

behaviours, 40, 83, 131, 139

Block, Peter, 142

blockers, 33, 69, 125, 126, 133

   resolving, 127

Brougham, Greg, 62

capabilities, 34, 70, 75, 128, 129

capability, 72, 79, 81, 116, 134, 140

   reviews, 134, 139

capacity, 33, 72, 120, 125, 127, 130, 133, 136, 138, 140

Castellino, Mariette, 27

Celebration (exercise), 11, 13, 25, 115

challenge, 12, 25, 72, 79, 86, 138, 141

change, 5, 115, 117, 120, 136, 142

   as real work, 6, 117, 135

   evolutionary, 145

   in progress, 117, 118, 125, 126, 127, 136

   management approaches, 2, 63, 112

   ownership, 118

   process, 7, 112, 117, 120, 122, 125, 126, 127, 128, 138, 142

   sustaining, 6, 78, 108, 112, 134, 141

Changeban, 152

chaos (Cynefin), 53, 55, 61, 103, 104

clarity, 34, 75, 114, 115, 128

   of purpose, 2, 75

   Organise for clarity, speed, and mutual accountability (principle), 8, 114, 115

Clean Language, 26, 27, 28, 44, 107, 109, 141

clean questions (Clean Language), 16, 20, 21, 27, 28, 42, 44

   Is there a relationship between X and Y?, 28, 44

   Is there anything else about X?, 16

   Then what happens?, 16, 18, 19, 43, 71, 105, 119, 141, 150

   What happens before X?, 16, 19

   What is happening when X?, 16, 19

   What kind of X?, 16, 20, 21, 43

   What would you like to have happen?, 16, 18, 19, 71, 118, 141, 150

client, 16, 18, 21, 43, 44, 107, 138

coach, 4, 16, 18, 20, 21, 27, 43, 44, 79, 105, 107, 138

coaching, 9, 27, 28, 35, 142

   exercise, 15

   frameworks, 107, 138

   relationship, 29, 138

   routines, 109

coherence, 74, 77, 86, 134, 141

collaboration, 33, 71, 72, 73, 118, 128, 129, 135, 141, 149

comfort zones, 4, 54, 62

commitment, 33, 71, 78, 132, 143, 144

   strategic, 145

communities, 145

   Agendashift, 58

   Agile, 106

   Clean Language, 27, 153

   Lean, 93, 107, 108

   Lean Startup, 124

   Lean-Agile, 3

   of practice, 144

completion, 134, 135

   focus, 33, 72, 125, 126, 128

complex (Cynefin), 53, 54, 56, 61, 91, 105, 107

complex systems, 61, 100, 146

complexity science, 61

complicated (Cynefin), 53, 54, 61, 99, 103, 104

confidence, 34, 70, 104, 126

consultants, 4, 21, 58, 96, 117, 135

context, 1, 2, 5, 13, 19, 35, 81, 91, 108

continuous delivery, 132

continuous improvement, 5

continuous transformation, 5, 112, 114, 115, 128, 138, 141, 142

contradictions, 72, 140

conversations, 3, 7, 14, 15, 16, 26, 76, 138, 141

   circular, 43

Cooper, Lynne, 27

coordination, 69, 97

corporate, 26, 45

   reputation, 55, 100

countermeasure, 103

Covey, Stephen, 1

cue card (15-minute FOTO), 20, 28, 43, 44, 151

culture, 54, 57, 141, 142, 144

customer, 72, 131, 133

   deliveries, 132

   dissatisfaction, 73

   expectations, 70, 130

   feedback, 34, 71, 133

   needs, 34, 75, 114, 128

   responsiveness, 70, 130

   satisfaction, 12

   support, 133

   value, 71

   wellbeing, 55

Customer focus, 34, 71, 118, 149

customer-first agenda, 133, 134

customers, 1, 12, 23, 72, 75, 97, 101, 130, 136

   unhappy, 131

Cynefin, 61

   domains, 53, 56, 61, 91

   Four Points contextualisation exercise, 45, 61, 103

   Four Points contextualisation exercise, debriefing, 53

   framework, 61

   pronunciation, 62

daily standup. *See* standup meetings

debrief, 35, 53, 118

decision making, 3, 121, 133

decisions, 34, 70, 102, 115, 121, 127, 129, 131, 133

Decisions, 114

delay, 14, 94, 127, 130

delegation, 48, 57, 104, 114

deliverables, 83

delivery, 33, 71, 115, 116, 140

continuous, 132

incremental, 130, 143

manager, 133, 143

planning meeting, 132

process, 23, 33, 34, 69, 72, 73, 117, 125, 129, 130, 132, 133, 142, 143, 145

systems, 34, 70, 75, 129

teams, 133, 134

Delivery planning meeting (Kanban), 132

demand, 72, 81

   quality, 73

dependencies, 34, 73, 80, 97, 127

   unresolved, 127

design

   choices, 136

   feedback loops, 146

   organisation, 115, 145

   solution, 1, 144

   system, 146

diagnosis, 19, 24, 44, 86

digital

   projects, 143, 144

   services, 90, 145

   strategy, 144

direction, 24, 26, 75, 79, 142, 143

disagreement, 39, 40, 41

disconfirmation (Schein), 141

discovery, 11, 23, 44, 56, 71, 85, 86, 107, 113, 114, 115, 135, 137, 138

disorder (Cynefin), 53, 61 dissatisfaction, 24, 68, 73

diversity, 91

domains. See Cynefin

downside (risk), 100

dysfunction, 24, 142

effectiveness, 33, 117, 118, 128, 146

efficiency, 71

   flow, 130

resource, 130

Elaboration, 89, 113, 115, 135, 136

empathy, 74, 139

engagement, 4, 91

  coaching, 138

  model, 138

enquiry, 27

  Appreciative, 107

  narrative, 61

evidence, 32, 84, 124, 134, 142

evolution, 5, 105, 143, 145, 146

execution, 54, 55, 98, 104, 105, 106, 110

expectations, 34, 70, 112, 127, 130, 144

experience

  service, 68, 70, 81

  shared, 144

  user, 144

experience before explanation, 9, 26, 32

experiments, 55, 57, 98, 109, 113, 114, 136

  developing, 106, 111

  framing, 106

  in progress, 126, 127

  managing, 142

  pilot, 98, 99, 101, 102, 104, 122, 127, 136

  tracking, 122

exploration, 31, 44, 78, 85, 86, 113, 115, 135,137

Facebook, 89, 94

facilitation, 21, 23, 25, 28, 37, 70, 74, 113, 139

  agreement, 42

  patterns, 59, 91

fail fast, 121

failure, 55, 79, 94, 98, 121, 144

fantastic (options, Roger L. Martin), 92, 93, 97, 99, 100, 105

feasibility, 121, 124, 136

Featureban, 152

features, 82, 143

  untested, 130

feedback, 71, 78, 130, 133, 135, 136, 138

  customer, 34, 71, 72, 133

feedback loops, 43, 129, 130, 132, 139, 145, 146

fitness for purpose, 68, 74, 81

flow, 34, 37, 70, 73, 81, 126, 127, 135, 143, 149

flow efficiency, 130

follow-through, 2, 34, 53, 75, 102, 112, 129, 134, 138

FOTO. *See* 15-minute FOTO

Four Points. See Cynefin Four Points contextualisation exercise

frameworks, 4, 138

  Agile, 2, 4, 26, 69, 134, 144

  coaching, 107, 109, 138

frustration, 24, 26, 73, 130

Full Circle (exercise), 149

Future, Backwards (Snowden), 25

Gall, John, 146

game, 29

games, 15, 19

  serious, 24

  time travel, 24

GDS. *See* Government Digital Services

generative, 2, 42, 137

goals, 21, 31, 44, 56, 82, 83, 86, 105, 109, 114, 140, 142, 143

  prioritised, 71, 129

  shared, 34, 71, 83, 128, 129

  strategic, 3, 138

Government Digital Services (GDS), 90, 144

  design principles, 144

Grove, David, 27

Harnish, Verne, 63

histograms, 36

Hohmann, Luke, 24

holding pattern, 127

hypotheses, 90, 109, 113, 136

  developing, 96

  framing, 111, *See*

  template, 94

hypothesis-driven change, 93, 109, 136

  alternatives to, 103

imagination, 2, 14, 26, 43, 115, 137

impact, 3, 18, 34, 40, 71, 83, 87, 114, 121, 128, 129, 131, 136

  external, 14

  isolation, 126

  observable, 94

  organisational, 145

  people, 36, 101, 121

  quantifying, 99

Impact Mapping, 83

impediments, 34, 73, 98, 127

improvement, 5, 32, 34, 53, 70, 75, 78, 81, 94, 95, 99, 103, 108, 112, 117, 127

  ideas, 34, 72, 75, 128, 129, 133

  opportunities, 34, 75, 81, 128, 129

  service, 12

  service experience, 68, 70, 81

  tracking, 54

incremental delivery, 130, 143

individuals, 13, 45, 59, 74, 139, 141, 142

  scale up from, 7, 14, 26, 137

influencers, 12, 101

innovation, 56, 144, 145

Innovation Games, 24

insights, 44, 55, 102, 121, 122, 125, 133, 136

inspect and adapt (Agile), 5

intent, 35, 68, 114

inventory, 130, *See also* work in progress (WIP)

invitation, 2, 22, 25, 43, 112

Is there a relationship between X and Y? (clean question), 28, 44

Is there anything else about X? (clean question), 16, 20, 21

iteration, 81, 105, 130, 135, 144

job stories, 83, 137

Jojic, Dragan, 57

judgement, 19, 22, 44, 94, 124

just-in-time (JIT) (Lean), 26, 93, 136

kanban, 126, 134

  board, 120, 123, 127

  systems, 81, 142

Kanban, 108, 131, 132, 152

  method, 143

Kanban from the Inside, 1, 7, 57, 62, 129, 141, 145

Keep the agenda for change visible (principle), 7, 113, 114

Keogh, Liz, 62

knowledge, 4, 90, 126

  bodies of, 3, 93, 97

  discovery process, 68, 71, 81

  work, 108

Lafley, A. G., 92

landscape, 31, 44, 113, 139

Lawley

  James, 28

lead time, 143

leader-leader (Marquet), 146

leadership, 4, 24, 34, 107, 142, 145, 149

  6 strategies (model), 78, 151

  at every level, 146

  principles, 79, 112

Lean, 3, 5, 26, 57, 72, 84, 93, 96, 105, 107, 133, 134, 135, 152

  20th and 21st century, 108

  change management (Little), 63

  pillars, 25

  strategy deployment, 63

Lean Startup, 93, 105, 120, 124, 143, 152

Lean-Agile, 7, 25, 69, 131, 133, 135

  change, 4

  process, 135

  sensibilities, 86

  transformation, 151

learning, 101, 105, 114, 121, 122, 141, 142, 144, 145

  opportunities, 71

  process, 126, 141

Learning organisation (Senge), 62

limits. *See* work in progress (WIP) limits

Little, Jason, 63

Manage options, testing assumptions (principle), 8, 113, 114

management systems, 109, 141
  visual, 81
managers, 26, 55, 79, 89, 101, 105, 133, 134
mapping, 31, 67, 86, 113, 115, 135, 136
Marquet, L. David, 146
Martin, Roger L., 92
Maurya, Ash, 106
McCandless & Lipmanowicz, 60
McKergow & Jackson, 108 Meadows, Donella ("Dana"), 146 meaning, 13, 26
meaningful, 77
meetings, 15, 17, 69, 97, 131, 133, 134, 139, 140
  Delivery planning (Kanban), 132
  Operations review (Kanban), 130, 133
  planning, 132, 139
  Release planning (Scrum), 132
  Retrospective (Scrum), 125
  Service delivery review, 133, 134, 139
  Sprint planning (Scrum), 126, 132
  Sprint retrospective (Scrum), 134
  Sprint review (Scrum), 134
  standup, 17, 58, 125, 127, 132, 133, 139
mentor, 105
metaphor, 20, 27, 108
metrics, 58, 75, 134, 140
mission, 140
models, 5, 7, 28, 78, 81, 85, 86, 130, 131, 135, 138, 146
motivation, 13, 23, 68, 73, 81, 139
mutual accountability, 8, 78, 79, 114, 129, 134, 138, 140, 146
narrative
  enquiry, 61
  flow, 68, 80
  micro-narratives, 41
needs, 26, 34, 56, 75, 78, 82, 129, 130, 135, 145
  anticipated, 1, 6, 7, 14, 78, 112, 137

authentic situation of need, 83, 140
  awareness, 112
  changing, 144
  discovering, 114, 140
  exploring, 78
  meeting, 26, 33, 55, 71, 72, 78, 83, 117, 128
  met, 2, 3, 7, 12, 14, 34, 72, 83, 118
  prioritising, 78, 140
  Start with needs (principle), 138, 144
  strategic, 23, 112, 138
  understanding, 23, 118
  versus requirements, 26, 83
Needs
  Start with needs (principle), 7, 113, 114, 144
negotiation, 120, 124, 127
non-prescriptive, 2, 3, 4, 7, 139, 144, 145, 149
objectives, 3, 21, 22, 138
observer, 16, 21
  outside, 12, 54
obstacles, 2, 4, 15, 16, 18, 20, 42, 43, 44, 71, 73, 75, 77, 86, 107, 109, 113, 115, 118, 126, 127, 137, 138, 140, 150
  exploring, 18
  specific, 15
  to outcomes, 15, 18, 21, 42, 70, 71, 73, 75, 118, 137
  to solution ideas, 43
obvious (Cynefin), 53, 57, 61, 99, 103
  The "obvious" question, 53
Odigeo, 127
Operation, 111, 135, 136, 138
Operations review meeting (Kanban), 130, 133
opportunities, 4, 21, 22, 23, 26, 42, 86, 98, 99, 111, 118, 125, 129, 134, 135, 136, 137, 138
  agreement on, 41
  alignment, 134
  delivery, 132
  frequent, 133
  identifying, 6

improvement, 34, 75, 81, 128

learning, 71

prospecting for, 31

urgent, 76

options, 15, 92, 113, 136, 138

fantastic (Roger L. Martin), 92, 93, 97, 99, 100, 105

generating, 91, 107, 111, 114

Manage options, testing assumptions (principle), 8, 113, 114

prioritisation, 114

selecting, 92

Options, 90

organisation, 116, 131, 133, 134, 142

design, 115, 145

scaling across and beyond, 7, 13, 14, 26, 112, 122, 137

scope, 56

structure, 12, 142

Organise for clarity, speed, and mutual accountability (principle), 8, 114, 115

outcome-oriented, 3, 25, 115, 141

outcomes, 1, 2, 43, 44, 45, 58, 69, 70, 76, 83, 86, 90, 105, 109, 115, 126, 127, 136, 137, 138, 140, 149

abstract and specific, 20

actionable, 79

Agree on outcomes (principle), 7, 113, 114

chain of, 18, 43, 71, 119, 126, 127

enabling, 80

exploring, 27

from obstacles, 15, 18, 21, 42, 70, 71, 73, 75, 118, 137

generating, 18, 21, 42, 70, 73, 75, 119

meaningful, 94

organising, 45

prioritisation, 79, 137

ranking, 76

realising, 140

short term, medium term, long term, 21, 56

thematic, 43

outside-in, 133, 134, 140

overburdened, 33, 38, 72, 125

ownership, 72, 118

participation, 2, 22, 35, 98, 133, 141, 142

overlapping, 133, 140

senior staff, 134

patterns, 26, 29, 127, 139, 141

facilitation, 59, 91

Patton, Jeff & Economy, Peter, 82

PDSA (or PDCA) cycle, 106

People and interactions over processes and tools (Agile manifesto), 4

performance, 34, 70, 116, 127

verification, 121

personas, 82, 83

perspectives, 1, 2, 82, 133, 136, 140, 145

Philip, Matt, 57

pilot experiments, 98, 99, 101, 102, 104, 122, 127, 136

planning, 22, 31, 54, 99, 105, 110, 131, 133, 135, 136, 139, *See also* meetings

project, 130

strategic, 63

plan-on-a-page, 22, 56, 63, 78

PMBOK, 93, 97

PMI, 93

policies, 103, 128, 144

guiding, 86

potential, 24, 92, 100, 101, 106, 114, 143

Powers, Simon, 62

POWT, 71, 118

practice-based assessment, 58

practices, 105, 149

prescribed, 2, 58

predictability, 71

prediction, 34, 70, 126

prescription, 1, 2, 3, 57, 58, 91, See also non-prescriptive

principles, 1, 3, 7, 25, 26, 35, 79, 93, 108, 112, 114, 115, 138, 144

Agendashift, 112

priorities, 22, 34, 42, 57, 71, 79, 111, 114, 120, 135, 138

prioritisation, 76, 113, 114, 119, 131, 136

proactivity, 6, 34, 73, 112, 134

problems, 26, 34, 75, 127, 128, 129, 131
quality, 71
responsibility, 91
underlying, 15

process, 2, 78, 116
culture formation, 141
design, 3, 130
evolution, 143, 144
flow, 12
improvement, 90, 117
Lean-Agile, 135
linear, 87, 105

product, 23, 24, 55, 130, 133
backlog (Scrum), 132
development, 82, 90, 105, 114
manager, 89, 133

product/process duality, 106, 117, 142

progress, 3, 26, 98, 99, 107, 114, 120, 125, 128, 132, 134, 144
reviews, 130

projects, 12, 13, 25, 54, 93, 130, 144
digital, 143, 144
time-bound transformation, 5

prompts, 35, 71, 86, 114, 117, 126, 127, 149
IDs, 43, 45, 69, 77

pull systems (Lean), 57, 72, 125, 128, 135

purpose, 2, 23, 68, 75

Purpose, 79

push. *See pull systems* (Lean)

quality, 2, 38, 94, 145
compromises, 130
movement, 105
of demand, 73
problems, 71

Rally Inc, 63

recognition, 34, 75, 128, 129, 139

reconciliation, 78, 84, 86

Rees, Judy, 27

reflection, 42, 74, 104, 137, 139

reject fast, 121

relationships, 27, 28, 29, 44
broken, 131
causal, 19, 104
coaching, 138

Release planning meeting (Scrum), 132

Remember the future (Innovation Games), 24

Replenishment/commitment meeting (Kanban), 132

reporting structures, 145

representation, 133, 140
customer, 133

reputation, 55, 98, 100

requirements, 26, 78, 83, 130
thinking, 83

resistance, 2, 58, 75, 135

resource efficiency, 130

resources, 28, 58, 62, 78, 96, 107, 151

Respect for people (Lean pillar), 4

responsibility, 34, 75, 79, 91, 114, 128

responsiveness, 70, 139

Retrospective meeting (Scrum), 125

Reverse STATIK (Kanban), 81

review, 34, 38, 54, 75, 78, 114, 121, 126, 128, 129, 133, *See also* meetings
blockers, 133
capability, 134, 139
kanban board, 125, 132
obstacles, 15
outcomes, 21, 76
post project, 131
progress, 130
prompts, 35, 42
requirements, 130
right-to-left, 125, 132, 134, 135, 140
risk, 101
scores, 35
strategy, 135

rewards, 34, 75, 128, 129, 139, 142

Ries, Eric, 106

Right conversations, right people, best possible moment, 7, 14, 26, 78, 137 right-to-left (review), 125, 132, 134, 135, 140

risk, 34, 70, 100, 126, 134

roles, 29, 33, 73, 128, 129

Rother, Mike, 108

Rumelt, Richard, 86

safe to fail (experiments), 100

safety, 28, 78, 100, 102, 103, 115

scale (organisation), 7, 13, 14, 26, 112, 122, 137

scale (scoring), 32, 33, 107, 118

Schein, Edgar H., 141

scope, 13, 22, 35, 41, 56, 78, 96, 136, 138

scores, 35, 126, 127

Scotland, Karl, 25, 63, 85

scribe, 16, 20, 43

Scrum, 4, 126, 132, 134, 143

Scrumban, 143

senior staff, 75, 117, 133, 134

sensemaking, 61

sequencing, 76, 127, 136

service, 23, 24, 55, 56, 130
    digital, 145
    experience, 68, 70, 81
    improvement, 12

Service delivery review meeting, 133, 134, 139

Shook, John, 107

skills, 22, 78, 79, 127

sliders, 58

Snowden & Boone, 62

Snowden, Dave, 25, 61, 62

society, 23

solutions, 1, 4, 26, 69, 104, 124
    complex, 112, 146
    design, 144
    ideas, 43
    multiple kinds, 91
    over-specified, 130
    potential, 141
    prematurely-specified, 15, 21

Solutions Focus, 107

sources of dissatisfaction, 81

sponsors, 4, 35, 58, 138

spread (of survey scores), 38, 39, 58

Sprint (Scrum), 132
    backlog, 132
    planning meeting, 126, 132
    retrospective meeting, 134
    review meeting, 134

staff, 1, 114, 131
    senior, 75, 101, 117, 133, 134

stakeholders, 14, 23, 72, 75, 114

standup meetings, 17, 58, 125, 127, 132, 133, 139

Start with needs (principle), 7, 113, 114, 138, 144

start with what you do now, 81, 107, 140

Start with what you do now, 1, 112, 146

starvation, 38, 94

STATIK (Kanban), 81
    Reverse, 81

story mapping. See User story mapping

strategic
    commitment, 145
    goals, 3, 138
    needs, 23, 112, 138
    planning, 63
    values, 144

strategy, 3, 6, 84, 86, 132, 134, 135
    digital, 144
    reviews, 139

Strategy Deployment (Lean), 63, 84

strategy kernel (Rumelt), 86

success, 12, 13, 24, 55, 78, 93, 94, 97, 98, 99, 120, 143, 144
    long term, 75
    measures of, 75

Sullivan & Rees, 27

suppliers, 12, 144

support, 34, 75, 114, 128, 129, 134

Surbek & Smalley, 107

surveys. *See Agendashift assessments*

sustainability, 6, 14, 78, 108, 112, 130, 134, 139, 141

sustainable pace (Agile), 72

swimlanes (kanban board design), 123

systems, 131

   complex, 146

   work management, 68, 81

Systems Dynamics, 146

Systems Thinking, 62, 145

Systems Thinking Approach to Implementing Kanban (STATIK), 81

TASTE (model), 85

teams, 7, 11, 12, 14, 26, 35, 70, 78, 105, 128, 130, 134, 137, 139, 144

   delivery, 133, 134

   frustration, 73

   policies, 128

technical debt, 130

testing, 57, 82, 94, 102, 118, 130

   assumptions, 8, 55, 71, 98, 99, 113, 114, 136

   hypothesis, 102

   thinking, 6, 104, 135

   user, 143

thematic outcomes, 77

themes, 56, 114, 137

Then what happens? (clean question), 16, 18, 19, 43, 71, 105, 119, 141, 150

thinking, 5, 6, 104, 135

time

   and space, 27

   horizons, 72, 78, 134

timeboxing, 126, 132

Tomkins

   Penny, 28

tools, 69, 138

Toyota, 93, 105, 108

Toyota Kata (Rother), 108, 134

tracking

   experiments, 122

   improvements, 54

transformation, 5, 78, 84, 86, 114

   continuous. *See continuous transformation*

process, 135

   rationale, 22

transformation map, 86, 119, 136, 137

Transformation Map, 31, 67

transparency, 138

   mutual, 134

Transparency, 32, 69, 114, 118, 145, 149

triangle, Organisation/Product/Process, 24, 116

True North, 7, 25, 85, 115, 151

UK government, 143, 144

understanding, 1, 23, 33, 34, 41, 54, 70, 71, 75, 76, 79, 86, 91, 104, 127, 136, 137

unlearning (Schein), 141

upside (risk), 100

upstream, 23, 136

urgency, 71, 76, 120

usability, 124, 136

user

   experience (UX), 144

   needs, 144

   research, 133

   testing, 143

user stories, 82, 137

User Story Mapping, 68

validation, 78, 97, 113, 136, 140

validation, 121

Valuable, Feasible, Usable, 124

value, 34, 70, 124, 126

values, 3, 5, 7, 21, 23, 57, 69, 75, 86, 131, 134, 139, 140, 142, 149

   strategic, 144

values-based, 141

vicious and virtuous circles, 43, 139, 145

visibility, 7, 33, 53, 69, 77, 113, 114, 117, 118, 121, 127, 141, 142

vision, 137

visualisation, 6, 56, 58, 76, 113, 135

Walker, Caitlin, 26, 28

Webber, Emily, 145

What else?, 105

What happens before X? (clean question), 16,

What has worked elsewhere?, 126

What is happening when X? (clean question), 16, 19

What kind of X? (clean question), 16, 20, 21, 43

What would experts from different backgrounds recommend?, 126

What would you like to have happen? (clean question), 16, 18, 19, 71, 118, 141, 150

Who, what, when, where, why (5W), 11

WIP. *See* work in progress

work in progress (WIP), 33, 69, 72, 81, 117, 118, 125, 132, 134
    limits, 126, 127

work items, 33, 69, 72, 117, 137
    blocked, 33, 69
    ownership, 34, 72
    types, 71, 72

work management systems, 69

workload, 38, 126, 133, 140

workshops, 6, 139, 151

X-matrix (Lean), 83

CPSIA information can be obtained
at www.ICGtesting.com
Printed in the USA
LVHW012351061218
599584LV00008B/254/P